FREEDOM FROM RELIGION

FREEDOM FROM RELIGION

NOEL MCGIVERN

To order additional copies of this book, contact:
Xlibris LLC
800-056-3182
www.Xlibrispublishing.co.uk
Orders@Xlibrispublishing.co.uk
307316

CONTENTS

Acknowledgements

I would like to thank Dr Paul Willis, Director of the Royal of Institution of Australia (RIAUS), for his advice on my chapter on evolution and his encouragement. I'm very grateful to Melissa Robson for producing such a striking cover. I have gained greatly from those who have engaged with me on Twitter, with courtesy (though not the trolls), and thank them for inspiration. I'd like to thank my wife, Carole, for reading and advising on my text and for her forbearance. And finally, I'd like to thank my New Zealand Huntaway dog, Becky, who plays her own special part in this book.

Introduction

'What you Atheists don't understand is that religion is about experience, it goes beyond rational arguments, and it is deeper than thought.' This sums up the case often made for religion. It claims to appeal to an authority beyond mere thought, declares itself as the gatekeeper to the eternal, and often thinks those claims give it rights over, at least, a section of humanity. Worse than that, religious believers often see those who don't conform to their doctrines, dogmas, or philosophies as ill-fated, evil, or damned, or in many cases all three.

Most arguments between believers and non-believers come down to a clash between, on one side, a rational argument and, on the other, an argument which seeks to counter with a rational approach but ultimately relies on the experiential or assertions of faith or belief, a distinction which is questionable.

This book goes beyond the normal intellectual territory of 'New Atheism'. It both explains the rational arguments against religion and examines the harm it does but, also, goes deep into the heart of the experiential claims often made for religion. It uses experience to directly question the validity of the spiritual claims of faith and how that experience is used as a source of authority in human society. Not least, amongst those claims, is the assertion that religion is the source of morality.

The falsity of the assumption that religion makes people good is explained, explored, and exposed. The excuses religions make are laid bare. Prominent among these is the answer to why religions have no grounds to claim that the violence, found in intercommunal conflicts, and other acts of violence, where religious identity plays a part, have nothing to do with religion. This book does not just examine these beliefs. It addresses the nature of religious identity itself and why it is the source of so much conflict.

It would be bad enough if terrible conflicts were the only harms of religion, but there is more to address, some of which is so very dark and distressing. There has been the Catholic Church's reckless and culpable irresponsibility over child abuse and the rapprochement between it and the Nazis. That is a reason to reflect on the wider responsibility Christianity, as a whole, shares for encouraging the anti-Semitic attitudes of those directly responsible for the atrocities, carried into concentration camps. My argument would not be enhanced by graphic details on any of these issues. The case against religion is strong enough without them.

The question of religious harm is not confined to the harms of Christianity. How Islam is used to oppress women, in Saudi Arabia, and how jurisdictions use it as an excuse to persecute Atheists are also addressed. The role of Christopher Hitchens, in the row over The Satanic Verses, is contrasted to the attitudes of Christian leaders who sided with those who put faith before freedom.

This book is addressed to those who have no personal experience of religion but wish to be equipped with clear arguments against it, to those who have already left religion and are seeking arguments that demonstrate the wisdom of having done so, and to those who are still within religion but are questioning its value. This book draws on a long journey through religion and spirituality and explains how seeking deep self-honesty led to a rejection of those ideas and beliefs.

I have, on a number of occasions, been indignantly asked by believers why I think anyone would need freedom from religion. They react as if I was suggesting that people needed freedom from health or happiness. They are convinced that the only true health and happiness can be found in spirituality. The recipe they often insist is necessary is often remarkably in accord with their specific brand of religiosity. Yet they often see no contradiction in asserting that religion is a universal need, while quite happily believing in a God or religion that excludes the great majority of humanity from the true health and happiness their brand of spirituality supposedly offers.

The logic of their position is that it is a person's own fault if they are careless enough to be born into the wrong religion or if they are so enthralled by reason that they reach a mental position where they can no longer believe in God. This attitude is by no means limited to the big theistic faiths of Christianity and Islam. It also appears to be very careless if you have allowed yourself to be born without the right karma for enlightenment or in families with the wrong moral character, as in many Eastern religions. The assumption of those horrified by the idea of freedom from religion, from these various religions, is that religion is essential, not just for your eternal destiny but also for moral character.

If, by the time you have read this book, you still think religion is mostly a force for good, you will either be someone with an extraordinary capacity for ignoring facts or simply not care about the harm religion does. Not only does this book test religion's claim to be the source of morality, but it demonstrates how, in many ways, it can and often does distort human morality.

This book examines why religious identity has a role in so many conflicts. It examines why religion is often the source of the darkest of human emotions. It looks at how the interests of religion have been put before needs and rights, while it has increased rather than diminished suffering.

It is also important to show that the claims of religion simply don't make sense. There are those who still believe in Adam and Eve, and in Noah's Ark. They deserve to have the problems with those beliefs laid out before them. How else can they walk away from them? The same goes for evolution and claims of a young Earth. These topics are more fully addressed elsewhere, but this book would not fulfil its remit if it failed to address them.

Some of you, who read this book, will have first encountered me on Twitter. I am aware that this world can be busy. I love Gibbon's Decline and Fall of the Roman Empire (well, he is wonderfully critical of Christianity), but my edition runs to eight volumes (I think the original may have been six). Anyway, the point is he does go on a bit. Twitter has taught me to be succinct. I imagine you reading this book on a train or tube or snatching a few minutes at lunchtime or between appointments, before classes, at last when the children have gone to sleep or at some other convenient juxtaposition, between the demands of your social, personal, or work life. So I have not allowed this work to ramble on too much.

To those of you who have not encountered me, 'Hi.' I promise you one thing about this book: it isn't boring. Some of you may strongly agree with it, while others may suddenly be struck with the realisation that the one great failing with e-books is you just can't hurl the wretched volume across the room. (Paper copies can be acquired for that purpose!)

Humans have a capacity to find humour, even in the darkest of topics. It is sometimes the only way we have to defy authority and express our humanity. This book is a manifesto for human freedom. It uncompromisingly addresses the harm and exposes the absurdities of religion. It does so to proclaim one simple right: the right to walk away from religion.

THE HARM OF RELIGION

Chapter One

WHY WOULD ANYONE WANT TO BE FREE FROM RELIGION?

Ah, but what of freedom? After all, 'Religion is freedom!' 'It's the greatest freedom anyone can have!' 'In Christ we are free!' 'The Prophet, peace be upon him, proclaimed humanity's greatest freedom, when he followed the guidance of the Angel Gabriel and wrote the Qur'an!' 'The Buddha set out the true path to freedom—the sevenfold path.'

Well, we can certainly say that there is no agreement among religions over what freedom religion is or brings. To be honest, we might as well throw in the lines:

> Freedom's just another word for nothing left to lose. ('Me and Bobby McGee' Lyrics © EMI Music Publishing, Warner/Chappell Music, Inc., Sony/ATV Music Publishing LLC)

Of course it's the Janis Joplin version I'm listening to, as I write. No one ever owned a song more than she owned 'Me and Bobby McGee'.

That, of course, is an opinion. Taste in music is a matter of opinion. This book is not about restricting opinions. It is against stating them as fact and imposing those supposed facts on others, especially when that involves oppressing those who disagree.

So what do I mean by freedom from religion? It is worth starting with the question: what it is in religion that people need to find freedom from?

There are people who are fortunate enough to have been brought up with no religion, in their childhood, but voluntarily enter one as adults. For them, religion is a free choice. The vast majority of people, however, are inducted into a religion in infancy. Should they, later in life, decide to reject their faith, most religions will regard them as apostates. The attitude towards those who do not believe is uncompromising in the New Testament.

> . . . those who do not believe are condemned already, because they have not believed in the name of the only Son of God. (John 3: 18)

To simply not believe is treated as intentional deviance. It is all that is required to secure a place in burning fires of damnation. This treats belief as a matter of wilful choice. But how can that be true? If you are a believer, I challenge you to test if belief can be a choice. If you are a Christian and are told that Islam is the only true way, can you simply decide that Islam is for you? If you are a Muslim, can you simply decide to be a Christian? I think you'll find you can't.

You can't do so because belief is not simply a matter of choice. To believe something, we must be convinced it is true. We can't make ourselves be convinced; we have to actually be convinced. To seek to make ourselves believe something we didn't would be intellectually dishonest. It would be to assert belief without conviction. How could we call that belief?

To not believe something is also a matter of intellectual honesty. It is to not be convinced the claims of that belief are true. Yet religions condemn people for that intellectual honesty, and they often condemn most strongly those who have come to the honest intellectual decision they can no longer believe in the claims of their religion. Those who voluntarily join a religion are treated with respect as converts; those who leave are contemptuously branded apostates.

> True Christians share Jehovah's feelings toward such apostates; they are not curious about apostate ideas. On the contrary, they 'feel a loathing' toward those who have made themselves God's enemies, but they leave it to Jehovah to execute vengeance. (Watchtower, 1 November 1993, p. 19)

The view of evangelical Christianity is expressed by the Canadian-born evangelical theologian and professor of New Testament Donald Arthur Carson.

> The universal witness of the New Testament is that apostasy if persisted in not only damns but shows that salvation was never real in the first place. The New Testament reveals how close one may come to the kingdom—tasting, touching, perceiving, understanding. And it also shows that to come this far and reject the truth is unforgivable. (D.A. Carson from Matthew, The Expositor's Bible Commentary)

Atheism is often the result of many years of sincerely reflecting on and examining religion. To sincerely question and conclude that religion makes no sense and is a cause of great harm to the world is in Professor Carson's eyes, unforgivable.

This professor regards honest intellectual inquiry, which does not come up with the results he agrees with, as unforgivable.

There are those who are convinced that the move from belief to non-belief is not the experience of intelligent questioning but a result of drifting into sin. John MacArthur, the pastor-teacher of Grace Community Church, Sun Valley, California, and president of The Master's College and Seminary, certainly sees it that way.

> No one sets out to become an apostate—it's never the result of one abrupt, drastic turn away from the Lord. Instead, apostasy is most often the product of a pattern of sinful compromises that harden and gradually steer a professing believer away from the truth. (John MacArthur, GTY Newsletter, 15 May 2009, www.gty.org)

We are being told that those who leave religion do so knowing that they are rejecting something of great value and they have made a series of sinful compromises. I have chatted with many fellow 'apostates' online from many countries and many different backgrounds. The most important reasons for leaving religion have been moral ones.

We have left religion because we came to a point where we saw it made no sense. Walking away was the only honest thing we could have done. In many cases, that was combined with an honest assessment that our religion, and quite often religion as a whole, does more harm than good. To walk away from harm and speak out against it, as many of us have done, is deeply moral. It has often been one of the most moral decisions we ever took in our lives.

Walking away from religion has often taken courage, the courage to be true to ourselves. Do those who attack us for it really think there would have been morality in continuing to adhere to a religion we no longer believe in? Where is the morality in remaining part of an institution we no longer have confidence in? Where is the morality in remaining silent about harm?

Yet we are often treated as traitors to a belief we did not consent to in the first place. How is that an attitude that respects freedom? Sometimes, religions protest that they grant us freedom. After all, the Qur'an says:

> There is no compulsion in religion. (Surah 2: 256)

Or

> Disbelievers! I do not worship what you worship nor do you worship what I worship. I shall never worship what you worship. You have your own religion and I have mine. (Surah 109: 1-6)

These would be some of the most laudable of sentiments in religion if there were not also many Surahs that say things like:

But [I have for you] only notification from Allah, and His messages.'
And whoever disobeys Allah and His Messenger—then indeed, for him is
the fire of Hell; they will abide therein forever. (Surah 72:23)

More controversially, it says:

They but wish that ye should reject Faith, as they do, and thus be
on the same footing (as they): But take not friends from their ranks until
they flee in the way of Allah (From what is forbidden). But if they turn
renegades, seize them and slay them wherever ye find them; and (in any
case) take no friends or helpers from their ranks. (Surah 4: 89)

This has been a matter of dispute amongst Islamic scholars. Whether the
punishment should be in this life or the next is not agreed on. However, this passage
has, on many occasions, been used to justify the punishment or execution of
apostates.

In recent times, there have been arrests for apostasy, usually accompanied
by allegations of blasphemy in Saudi Arabia and Indonesia. A report from The
Economist addressed the issue:

A MOB attacked Alexander Aan even before an Indonesian court in
June jailed him for two and a half years for 'inciting religious hatred'. His
crime was to write 'God does not exist' on a Facebook group . . .

In a handful of majority-Muslim countries atheists can live safely,
if quietly; Turkey is one example, Lebanon another. None makes atheism
a specific crime. But none gives atheists legal protection or recognition.
Indonesia, for example, demands that people declare themselves as one
of six religions; atheism and agnosticism do not count. Egypt's draft
constitution makes room for only three faiths: Christianity, Judaism and
Islam . . .

Potential sanctions can be severe: eight states, including Iran, Saudi
Arabia, Mauritania and Sudan have the death penalty on their statute
books for such offences.

In reality such punishments are rarely meted out . . . religion. Even in
places where laws are lenient, religious authorities and social attitudes can
be harsh, with vigilantes inflicting beatings or beheadings. (http://www.
economist.com/news/international/21567059-ex-muslim-atheists-are-
becoming-more-outspoken-tolerance-still-rare-no-god-not)

The persecution of people on the grounds of their religious belief is a deep
violation of basic human rights and so is the persecution of those who reject religion.
No one who defends freedom of religion can seriously claim to be proclaiming

a right unless they also defend the right to criticise or walk away from religion. Political and religious leaders in democratic countries often attack regimes that deny religious freedom. How often do you hear them defending the apostates?

In 1989, when a fatwa was issued against the writer Salman Rushdie, and his life was threatened, for his novel The Satanic Verses, his friend Christopher Hitchens wrote this in the New York Times article entitled: 'Now, Who Will Speak for Rushdie?' He criticised the absence of . . . bishops and rabbis and imams, denouncing the exploitation of piety for the ends of suppression, murder and torture . . . imagine how you would feel if you heard your death called for on the radio, and had to wonder about yourself and your family for the rest of your life. (New York Times, 17 February 1989, http://www.nytimes.com/1989/02/17/opinion/now-who-will-speak-for-rushdie.html)

Far from religious leaders defending Rushdie's freedom, many condemned him. Cardinal Archbishop O'Connor of New York called the book blasphemous. Robert Runcie, the Archbishop of Canterbury, backed calls to have the United Kingdom's blasphemy laws, which only protected Christianity, expanded to cover other religions, including Islam.

It is worth considering the morality of this situation. Christopher Hitchens was standing by a friend who had done no more than have the misfortune to write a novel that had been, on extremely tenuous grounds, interpreted as blasphemous. His friend, Salman Rushdie, had been threatened with death and had gone into hiding, for his own safety and that of his loved ones. Rushdie (Now Sir Salman Rushdie), who, at that stage, had not repudiated his Muslim faith, had merely written the account of the deluded dream of one of his characters. Democratic governments had equivocated; other writers had shown hesitation and even, in the case of Arthur Miller, expressed fear of making public statements defending Rushdie. Hitchens hadn't. His case is very eloquently put on a C-Span interview with Bruce Collins shortly after the fatwa against Salman Rushdie was issued by Ayatollah Ruhollah Khomeini of Iran (http://www.youtube.com/watch?v=kTeffd-xvBg).

Hitchens did not falter in his loyalty to a friend in need and made it clear he would equally defend the freedom of speech of those he disagreed with. Morality is meaningless without moral courage. Hitchens had showed moral courage.

Religion is proclaimed as the source of morality. The Anglican (Episcopalian) Archbishop of Canterbury and the Roman Catholic Cardinal Archbishop of New York had demonstrated an example of Christian unity. They had been in accord in lending legitimacy to the spurious, trumped up, and unfounded charge against Salman Rushdie. They had shown more concern for protecting religion, as a source of human authority, than with a man whose life had been threatened because of nothing more than an ill-informed interpretation of his novel. They had put religion before human rights and freedoms.

In truth, the Archbishops were reflecting a long-held Christian attitude towards apostasy and heresy. This is what the Catholic Encyclopaedia says:

> Apostasy belonged, therefore, to the class of sins for which the Church imposed perpetual penance and excommunication without hope of pardon, leaving the forgiveness of the sin to God alone . . .
>
> Today the temporal penalties formerly inflicted on apostates and heretics cannot be enforced, and have fallen into abeyance. The spiritual penalties are the same as those which apply to heretics. In order, however, to incur these penalties, it is necessary, in accordance with the general principles of canon law, that the apostasy should be shown in some way. Apostates, with all who receive, protect, or befriend them, incur excommunication . . . (http://www.newadvent.org/cathen/01624b.htm)

Yes, if you are a Catholic, simply befriending an ex-Catholic could cause you to be excommunicated. As if that is not bad enough, there are consequences for the children and some grandchildren of apostates. The article later states:

> They incur, moreover, the note of 'infamy', at least when their apostasy is notorious, and are 'irregular'; an infamy and an irregularity which extend to the son and the grandson of an apostate father, and to the son of an apostate mother, should the parents die without being reconciled to the church.

So, with a sexism that is hardly surprising, considering the Catholic Church's attitude towards the ordination of women, the sin of apostasy is treated more severely when it is supposedly committed by a man than by a woman. It is passed as an inheritance to the male offspring. The point is powerfully made, the Catholic Church officially treat the children and in some cases the grandchildren of apostates and heretics as tainted with evil.

I am fully willing to accept this is a case where the stated position of the Catholic Church often differs in theory and practice. These vindictive sanctions don't actually apply in most cases. But where the Catholic Church has chosen to exercise the sanction of excommunication and where it has declined to do so is even more shocking than this policy.

Adolf Hitler, whose relationship with the Vatican is addressed later, was never excommunicated from the church. He never publicly disavowed his Catholicism, and we have no grounds to believe other than that he would have been entitled to the full rites of the Roman Catholic Church until he died.

This contrasts with the excommunication of the mother and doctor of a nine-year-old girl in Brazil, in 2009, who'd had an abortion after she'd been raped, allegedly by her stepfather (http://news.bbc.co.uk/1/hi/world/americas/7930380.stm). Yes, the Catholic Church treated those seeking to protect the welfare of a severely abused nine-year-old girl as more worthy of excommunication than the terrible crimes of Adolf Hitler. Making a nine-year-old girl go full term with a pregnancy and allowing Adolf Hitler to remain a Catholic were the apparently the moral things to do.

Where exactly is the moral compass in this? When you look at a case like that how can you draw any other conclusion than the Catholic Church, and other religions, often regard human beings as their property? They see church members as born to serve them and dismissible when they deviate from doctrine or dogma of that church, and yet, have repeatedly shown terrible cowardice in the face of the most evil of tyrants?

That sense of being owned is often the aspect of religion that people most strongly wish to be free from. That is for the very good reason that it was inflicted upon so many of us without our consent. This is not simply a question of an infant induction into a faith by a ceremony such as baptism. Even confirmation in Christian churches and bar mitzvah in Judaism, which are theoretically adult decisions, are usually carried out at an age where a child is still very much under parental control. What Catholic child is genuinely free to say no to confirmation? What Jewish boy, brought up in a devout family, could refuse his bar mitzvah, as though it were a library book he didn't want to read, and do so with impunity from familial pressure?

It is true that in some Baptist churches, the decision to be baptised is left until adulthood. While the reasons may be theological, it is, at least, a commendable approach. However, even in faiths which don't use such ceremonies, the childhood indoctrination of religious ideas is often very intense, and there is a need to find liberation from the dependency and dark fantasies that religion so often perpetuates.

This book is not an attack on freedom of worship or against the right to believe. It is, however, an analysis of the nature of religion, which exposes it as the nonsense and often great harm it is. However, just because ideas make no sense and cause harm does not mean banning them is a good idea. In the case of religion, it would be counterproductive, just as the prohibition of alcohol in the United States in the 1930s was counterproductive. The likely outcome would be it would reinforce religious identity, which is one of the most dangerous aspects of religion.

Frankly, you can't ban a belief because we have no power over what people think and nor should we have. More importantly, a free society should only restrict speech or other freedoms of expression where there is no other way to prevent serious harm. Governments have every right to, and should, prevent the spreading of child pornography, because of the deep harm caused by making such images. Banning and actively prosecuting those who create, promote, and possess such images is the only way to address that problem.

While there are grave problems with religion, the harm is very different in character. Much of religious activity is perfectly harmless. Attendance at a church, mosque, synagogue, or temple is not, in itself, a threat to anyone. In a free society, religion can and should be countered through free speech.

While many are introduced to a religion without either their knowledge or their consent, the rejection of a religion is best done by informed consent and as a free and intelligent decision. This contrasts sharply with the approach of most religions.

Chapter Two

Don't Humans Need Religion?

There is not only evidence that we Homo sapiens developed religious ideas early in our social development, but also evidence that Neanderthals, who appear to have died out around 30,000 years ago and whose DNA is still found in many modern humans, behaved in ways that could be termed religious.

> In the 1950s, Smithsonian anthropologist Ralph Solecki, a team from Columbia University and Kurdish workers unearthed the fossilized bones of eight adult and two infant Neanderthal skeletons—spanning burials from 65,000 to 35,000 years ago—at a site known as the Shanidar cave, in the Kurdistan area of northern Iraq. The discovery changed our understanding of Neanderthals . . .
>
> Solecki's pioneering studies of the Shanidar skeletons and their burials suggested complex socialization skills. From pollen found in one of the Shanidar graves, Solecki hypothesized that flowers had been buried with the Neanderthal dead. (http://www.smithsonianmag.com/arts-culture/The-Skeletons-of-Shanidar-Cave.html#ixzz2Y5Q2fTvD)

Later work suggested that the evidence of flowers may have been from the pollen left by gerbils that had infested the cave, which rather detracted from the romantic notion of flowers on the grave. That aside, the burials do show evidence of a belief system and that this earlier species had a need to cope with grief. They do not, however, show that religion is an intrinsic human need. Those who argue that ancient religions provide evidence that it is a fundamental human need should explain what that need is and which specific aspects of ancient religions reflect it.

Karen Armstrong explains the case for that need in Neolithic humans.

Religion was not something tacked on to the human condition, an optional extra imposed on people by unscrupulous priests. The desire to cultivate a sense of the transcendent may be the defining human characteristic. In 9000 BCE, when human beings developed agriculture and were no longer dependent on animal meat, the old hunting rites lost some of their appeal and people ceased to visit the caves [Lascaux caves]. But they did not discard religion altogether. Instead they developed a new set of myths and rituals based on the fecundity of the soil that filled the men and women of the Neolithic age with religious awe. (The Case for God, Karen Armstrong, Bodley Head, London, 2009, p. 19)

The first question is how does Karen Armstrong know that Neolithic people were filled with religious awe over the fecundity of the soil? That their life had a ceremonial aspect is indisputable. That does not mean they were any more in awe than the average modern churchgoer. She seems keen to want to imbue them with a collective fervour which goes beyond the evidence.

We are presented with a picture of the distant ancestors of modern Europeans who moved away from hunting rites and developed new rituals in an agricultural lifestyle. The Lascaux cave—in France, Montignac, in the department of Dordogne—was discovered in 1940 by four young boys who followed a dog called 'Robot' into the cave. Yes, a dog did discover one of the world's most important archaeological sites. They found incredible pictures of animals and symbols which had been created by Ice Age hunters. These include the image of a human figure wearing a bird-like mask standing next to a wounded bison. These pictures that depict a relationship between the hunter and prey show no evidence that humans were looking to any external authority to control that environment. The forces they depict are immediate to their lives.

They are wonderful paintings with tremendous vibrancy and are considered sacred. Yet there is no agreement over why they were sacred. Are they portraits of the initiation of young hunters? Was it a shamanic culture that emphasised sympathetic magic? It this case that would imply there was a belief that the painting of a successful hunter would lead to successful outcome on the hunting field. We could speculate that the bird's head symbolised a seeking of the power of a bird, in some way. The point is it is all speculation.

This is very different from later 'sacred' sites like the massive astrological monuments such as Stonehenge, in Wiltshire in the South of England. It has usually been assumed that this monument was built to celebrate the summer solstice. There is, however, an increasing view that it may have been built for the winter solstice, for which the solar alignment is equally valid.

As archaeologist Parker Pearson explains:

> The pigs were evidently slaughtered at midwinter, and he expects the cattle bones to back this. What the sample already tested shows is that they were slaughtered immediately after arrival, after travelling immense distances. (http://www.guardian.co.uk/culture/2009/dec/20/stonehenge-animal-bones-solstice-feast)

It seems highly probable that this and similar monuments were built to mark the dying and rebirth of the sun in winter. They may, of course, also, have marked midsummer. But the precise nature of the beliefs is again speculation.

Karen Armstrong argues that the transition from the hunting to pastoral culture, with astronomical monuments, shows evidence that a desire to cultivate a sense of the transcendent may be the defining human characteristic. Yet there is a much simpler explanation. It seems more probable that the mystical arose out of a human desire to control an environment they had no other explanation for. That there was a move from hunting rites to pastoral ones is more readily explained by the new need to appease the elements, they saw as controlling the climate and fertility of crops, than by an intrinsic mystical need for the transcendent. The cave paintings show only a desire to gain control of the prey because of the need to eat. That need to eat did not arise from a deep mysticism.

What humans did develop was imagination and creativity. They had needed to imagine the movements of the prey they stalked. Now they needed to imagine the outcome of planting seeds. Beyond that, where is the continuity in human spirituality? Where are the similarities that identify these two things as the same phenomenon?

That is not to deny that the mystical can be very powerful. It can be, as will be, examined later. However, there is nothing in these examples that suggests that it is anything more than a powerful by-product of the human imagination and the emotions that arise from its response to the environment which provides essential sustenance. We will later examine how that response can arise in times of crisis.

Normally, when we define human needs, we can define what those needs are and why they are needed. We need nutrition and water to maintain our body. We need human relationships for emotional and sexual needs. We need sunlight for vitamin D. These needs apply across all cultures. Therefore, we can class them as universal human needs. Those who wish to argue that religion is a fundamental human need should identify what that need fulfils and what it is in the character of religion that fulfils it. What are the elements in it that constitute a universal need? What are the common factors we find across all religions that meet those needs?

One argument is that humans have an intrinsic need to worship God. Yet most ancient religions were polytheistic (worshipping many gods). Hinduism is a modern example of a religion with aspects of this. Few monotheists (believers in one God) would argue that the worship of many gods is a fundamental human need. Not all religions worship a God. Buddhism, in its purer forms, doesn't. So, we can't say belief in God passes our test of a universal human need.

Another argument is that prayer is a fundamental need. Yet not all religions pray; some emphasise meditation. Plenty of non-believers manage to get through life without either. So there are no grounds to call prayers a universal need.

It is argued that religions have provided humans with a necessary form of leadership through the roles of priests, ministers, or other recognised religious leaders. However, not all religions have leaders. The Society of Friends (Quakers) believes in the priesthood of all believers and therefore has none.

There is evidence of child sacrifice in Aztec and Inca cultures. It is there in ancient Hebrew culture (we will address this later). We find it in Phoenicia and Carthage. The evidence of animal sacrifice is even more pervasive. Should we conclude that the sacrifice of living creatures, to appease a deity, is a fundamental human need?

What about monuments built to precise astronomical calculations? We find those across the globe. Is a monument to mark the solstices a fundamental human need?

We could say then an organisation that has clergy and churches and a membership who regularly attends them to worship, or any combination of these elements, is a religion. However, none of these elements is essential for the definition of a religion. So we can define certain organisations as religions, but it is a great deal more difficult and often impossible to define what is not a religion.

We can reasonably conclude that since the beliefs of religions are far too diverse to be definable and there is nothing in them we can define as a universal need, they can't be classed as a need.

There is, of course, one aspect of religion which is repeatedly presented as a human need. That is morality. How often are we told that humans need religion to provide morality? That is certainly a claim that needs to be examined and it will be.

Chapter Three

IT IS JUST POETRY

Back in the late 1970s, when platform shoes and flared trousers were all the rage, the pop band Boney M. sold nearly two million copies of the record 'Rivers of Babylon'. The tune was catchy, and the performance was polished, well as polished as anything in a Seventies disco could have been. It starts with a harmony and contains powerful and evocative lyrics like:

> Ye-eah we wept, when we remembered Zion. They carried us away in captivity requiring of us a song . . . Now how shall we sing the lord's song in a strange land? ('Rivers of Babylon' Lyrics © Royalty Network, EMI Music Publishing, Sony/ATV Music Publishing LLC, Universal Music Publishing Group)

But everything was not as it seemed. In my mind, I visualise the abrupt scratching of the stylus against the vinyl and the music tailing off as the record is abruptly stopped. That just won't work with an MP3, but it is the treatment this song deserves.

There were a number of problems with this record. For a start, the song gets its psalms mixed up:

> 'By the rivers of Babylon, there we sat down'

comes from Psalm 137, but the line:

> 'Let the words of our mouth and the meditation of our hearts be acceptable in thy sight here tonight'

is taken from Psalm 19.

That is no more than a quibble. But even in the 1970s, one or two DJs pointed out that there was a more serious problem with the song. There was the problem we did not discover until much later. Bobby Farrell, the male singer with band didn't actually perform on many of the records. The producer Frank Farian sang on them instead. What the band had done was picked a performer who looked good on stage, as the apparent band member, but used a stronger voice for recording. That was dodgy but there was something much more questionable going on. The problem was there was something missing from the song. There had been a judicious piece of editing.

As mentioned above, the song was largely based on Psalm 137. If you listen to the song, you'd think it was simply a lament of a captured people who have been taken far from their homeland. However, Psalm 137 is more than a song of homesickness. It contains, within it, an expression of extreme hatred. In fact, it has one of the most extreme expressions of hatred you'll find anywhere in the Bible. Not only did Boney M. not sing the last verse but that they could not have released a version of the song that included it. The last verse goes:

> Happy shall he be, that taketh and dasheth thy little ones against the
> stones. (Ps. 137: 9, King James Version (KJV))

What excuse can there be for treating a book with a statement like that as sacred? Well, believers do like to make excuses for the Bible. Funny, how even those who claim the Bible to be the infallible and inerrant word of God sometimes like to make excuses for it. I've heard many excuses in this case.

The excuses are well rehearsed. So let's examine what they are for this vile little verse. A much loved way of explaining away parts of the Bible is to say that there has been a mistranslation. Well, fair enough, let's try another version. Here's one of the more recent ones.

> Happy is the one who seizes your infants and dashes them against the
> rocks. (Ps. 137: 9, New International Version)

Now that version is, if anything, even clearer. No ambiguity of translation there. It actually says infants. In the interests of fairness, let's try the Tanach (the Jewish Bible).

ט. אַשְׁרֵי | שֶׁיֹּאחֵז וְנִפֵּץ אֶת עֹלָלַיִךְ אֶל הַסָּלַע:

This translates as:

> Praiseworthy is he who will take and dash your infants against the rock.

I think we can be certain we have a correct translation of Psalm 137.

Another much loved excuse of Bible apologists is that the text should be read with a soft heart. Believers are forever complaining that we non-believers are just too hard-hearted in our understanding of the Bible. OK. Let's try to be soft-hearted about calls to batter babies against rocks. Does that work for you? It certainly doesn't for me. It is something I hope to never be soft-hearted about. I oppose it with all my heart and hope you do too. But perhaps we should read this as poetry. Yes, believers have told me that is the correct approach. Think about that. Imagine a teacher setting a class a poetry writing task and telling the students to write a poem about dashing babies against rocks. Are you struggling with that one? Would you have a little difficulty with the metaphors? I have to say it doesn't work for me either.

However, it is poetical, in style, but how is that an excuse? To say something which is a public declaration is poetical is a very odd way of saying it is not meant to be taken as true. Martin Luther King's Address at the March on Washington on 28 August 1963, Washington, DC, with the highly powerful words 'I have a dream' used deeply poetical techniques. The speech of Churchill with the phrase 'We will fight them on the beaches' is also a deeply poetical use of language. These are two of the most important speeches of the twentieth century. The use of poetical techniques increases the power of these speeches. It makes them memorable; it made them inspiring.

The 137th Psalm is a carefully constructed piece of writing. Anyone with the most rudimentary knowledge of poetry will know how important last lines can be. This psalm starts by evoking powerful feelings of exile and injustice and ends in the most terrible declaration of hatred. There is nothing accidental about the psalm and certainly not about the ending. Its use of poetry cannot be used to defend it but is very much a part of the case for the prosecution against it.

'But that was back in biblical times. It was the Old Testament. Things were different.' How many times have you heard that excuse? Well, what is the logic of this argument? Did babies somehow suffer less back then? Were they less fragile?

One of the most loved excuses for unpleasant Bible passages is, 'You're reading it out of context.' OK. In precisely, what context is it OK to call for dashing babies against rocks? It will certainly increase our understanding if we explore the context for this psalm. To do so, we need look at a couple of other books of the Bible. We don't have an account of the exile in Babylon. However, like Psalm 137, they were written after the return from it.

THE BOOK OF EZRA

The Bible can be a very dull book, but I recommend that if you want to grasp the full horror of it, you read it from start to finish. I fully understand why many people would never contemplate doing so. Fortunately, for those who do, these days, audio versions of it on e-book readers can help. Whatever way, those of us who do read it, get through it; reading it all is hard work and takes determination.

By the time you read through the Second Book of the Chronicles (believe me one of them is more than enough), you have been through a lot of mindless violence, animal sacrifices, tedious details of temple building, and lists. It is hard to imagine how even the most devout fundamentalists could care about those many of those lists. They can be so tedious. After 2 Chronicles is the Book of Ezra. It has the advantage of being a short book, with only ten chapters.

Let me tell you about my experience of reading the Book of Ezra. I reached it thinking, at least it wouldn't take me long to get through it. I could tick off another book. I didn't expect it to be much of an improvement on 2 Chronicles, but I waded in. It has a list at the end, and I'd made up my mind not to miss out any of the lists, no matter how boring. But this wasn't a boring list. This list was heartbreaking. It was a list made, after the return from Babylon, of all the men who were deemed to have sinned because they had married foreign women. The book tells how they were made to divorce them.

> And they gave their hands that they would put away their wives; and being guilty, they offered a ram of the flock for their trespass. (Ezra 10: 19)

From Ezra 10: 20-43 is a list of all the men who had foreign wives. Then comes the last line.

> All these had taken strange wives: and some of them had wives by whom they had children. (Ezra 10: 44)

The book after Ezra is the Book of Nehemiah. In Chapter 13, the author explains how he expresses his anger at those who have taken foreign wives:

> And I contended with them, and cursed them, and smote certain of them, and plucked off their hair, and made them swear by God, saying, Ye shall not give your daughters unto their sons, nor take their daughters unto your sons, or for yourselves. (Neh. 13: 25)

This is a vile expression of racist hatred. It has sentiments comparable to the worst of racist thugs and of the hatred of the Nazis. Now let's return to the last line of Psalm 137:

> Happy shall he be, that taketh and dasheth thy little ones against the stones. (Ps. 137: 9)

It is not a metaphor. It is not just poetry. It is not something we can read with a soft heart. It is cruel racist hatred. We have a list in which the names of the fathers, of the children, at whom a similar hatred was aimed at, are included.

If anyone ever tells you they get their family values from the Bible, ask them to explain Psalm 137 and the Books of Ezra and Nehemiah. Ask them why the Bible approves of forcing men to abandon their wives and children and why it has a verse that wishes the children of their enemies dashed against rocks?

The Bible claims morality and yet it expresses hatred against Babylonian babies and against the offspring of marriages between Jews and any of the other peoples around them. There is no morality in believing in a god who demands such cruelty or who is believed to sanction such hatred against children.

Chapter Four

CHILD SACRIFICE

The idea of child sacrifice is usually seen as alien to the biblical account of God. It is portrayed as a practice of foreign religions who worshipped false gods. The attitude towards the possibility of it is often explained by the account of Abraham and Isaac in Genesis 21. Here an angel intervenes to prevent the murderous act. This story is recounted as an example of Abraham's great faith. Yet we should seriously question that.

Abraham was convinced that he heard the voice of God telling him to kill his son. Do we really think someone believing they have been told to kill by God is a good idea? Is it a sign of good mental health? This is dangerously psychopathic thinking. Do we think that such an idea should ever be given credibility? We have to understand that roots of theistic religion don't lie in peaceful contemplation but in men who are prepared to put their fanatical beliefs before anything or anyone else.

If we were to believe such a God existed, how could a deity who would cause that level of distress ever be worthy of worship? Wouldn't we have to conclude that only a very sadistic and cruel being would bring a man to the point of killing his own son and bring a son to the point of being convinced his father was about to kill him? It seems that most believers don't truly think about the cruel nature of that story.

This is not the only case in the Bible where God is portrayed as demanding child sacrifice. In Judges 11: 29-40, we find the account of Jephthah, one of Israel's judges (in effect a general) who made a vow to God that if he won a battle, he would sacrifice the first member of his household who came out to greet him on his return. Presumably, he hoped it would be a servant. However, on his return after his victory against the Ammonites, in which he had destroyed twenty cities, his daughter was the first to emerge from his house.

He was very distressed by this and reluctant to carry out his vow to God. He allowed her two months to go into the mountains, with her friends, and bewail her virginity. The Bible states

> And at the end of two months, she returned to her father, who did
> with her according to his vow which he had made. She had never known a
> man . . . (Judg. 11: 39)

The meaning of this text is unambiguous. Jephthah had made a vow to sacrifice
the first person who came out of his house and had kept it. Most believers are
unaware of this story, but those who know it have often tried desperately to argue it
doesn't mean what it says. The final verse says:

> The daughters of Israel went year by year to lament the daughter of
> Jephthah the Gileadite four days in the year. (Judg. 11: 40)

I have found Christians who give the contrived explanation that the daughters of
Israel lamented the continued virginity of the daughter of Jephthah, and therefore,
she wasn't killed at all. That would not have been keeping the vow. Moreover, people
mourn the dead and not the living. To invent a tradition of mourning a living person
smacks of desperation.

Child sacrifice was part of ancient Hebrew tradition. Had it not been, the
practice would not have been condemned again and again in the Bible. We find
references to it in many of the books from Genesis to Revelation. Sadly, the attitude
towards children of some in religious offices has continued to be a matter of grave
concern.

Chapter Five

MARRIAGE

The Christian claim is that marriage is an institution ordained and sanctioned by God. Christians, of course, differ over what this means. The Catholic Church does not permit divorce but allows annulment where the marriage is considered to be invalid for a variety of reasons. These reasons range from one party being unable to give consent, one party being deemed to have been psychologically unable to consent to the full obligations of marriage, or one party having omitted to mention they were in holy orders. (Well, anyone could forget a thing like that) One party not being baptised, where no dispensation was granted, is another get-out clause.

Most Protestant churches argue that divorce is undesirable but permissible in circumstances such as desertion, adultery, or cruelty.

There are a small minority of Christian churches who recognise gay marriage as valid. However, most of them define marriage as a lifelong union between one man and one woman and hope for that ideal to be upheld when a couple make their vows. They claim this definition is based on a definition of marriage decreed by God and found in the Bible. But is it?

> But King Solomon loved many strange women, together with the daughter of Pharaoh, women of the Moabites, Ammonites, Edomites, Zidonians, and Hittites: Of the nations concerning which the Lord said unto the children of Israel, Ye shall not go in to them, neither shall they come in unto you: for surely they will turn away your heart after their gods: Solomon clave unto these in love. And he had seven hundred wives, princesses, and three hundred concubines: and his wives turned away his heart. (1 Kgs. 11: 1-3)

So Solomon, that font of great wisdom in the Bible, had 700 wives and 300 concubines. He sinned. Obviously, he did, you might think. It was having all those wives and concubines. But no, having all those wives and concubines is not the sin the Bible records against him.

The sin of Solomon was that he built temples for the gods of his wives. He respected their religions. That is the sin Solomon is condemned for. The Bible does not say his polygamy was a sin.

Solomon's father King David was also polygamous and not just with the famed Bathsheba. He had seven wives. Many of the key figures in the Bible were powerful men who took many wives. So, monogyny was certainly not seen as the only acceptable union by the Old Testament God. And the commandment 'Thou shalt not commit adultery' did not mean there must be one man and one woman. What about the idea marriage should be for life?

As we have seen in the Books of Ezra and Nehemiah, the Old Testaments showed no respect for marriages that did not fit in with its politics. Those passing the racist marriage laws of South Africa or some Southern US states had no difficulty in finding justification in the Bible.

We can find references to monogamy in the New Testament. However, the position it takes is far from clear. Within a few verses, it starts saying that what God has joined together no one can pull apart.

> Wherefore they are no more twain, but one flesh. What therefore God
> hath joined together, let not man put asunder. (Matt. 19: 6)

A few verses later we find the loophole of the wife's adultery. Christianity is divided on whether to accept the first absolute ruling against divorce or the very useful loophole.

> Whosoever shall put away his wife, except it be for fornication, and
> shall marry another, committeth adultery. (Matt. 19: 9)

It is, therefore, not at all clear what Christians mean when they protest against same-sex marriage, on the grounds they are protecting the sanctity of marriage. They are arguing for a concept that has changed in the Bible and is defined in such self-contradictory terms that it certainly has no authoritative meaning.

The problem is that not only is their claim about marriage flawed, but there is evidence of a gay relationship between two great heroes of the Old Testament, David and Jonathan. It is denied by believers that it is anything more than a strong male friendship, but the text suggests more:

> I am distressed for thee, my brother Jonathan: very pleasant hast thou
> been unto me: thy love to me was wonderful, passing the love of women.
> (2 Sam. 1: 26)

Chapter Six

CHILD ABUSE

One of the most disturbing questions in religion is why loving parents would remain part of an organisation which has leaders who have actively protected child abusers. It is fair to point out that paedophilia is by no means unique to religion. The BBC has, in recent times, been rocked by the terrible revelations about how the late Jimmy Savile, a radio DJ and popular television presenter, rampantly abused young girls, and occasionally boys, for many years. Other radio and television personalities have been accused and, in some cases, convicted of similar crimes. The crimes have been just as serious, and the harm just as great as those Catholic priests have been guilty of.

However, there are key differences between the BBC and Catholic Church. The BBC does not behave as a moral guardian of Britain or the world; it doesn't claim spiritual authority over 1.3 billion people. It is not a primary human identity. Any organisation can have paedophiles in it, but what sets the Catholic Church apart is how actively it sought to protect them and itself.

Throughout history, churches have claimed the right to define what is good and evil. The treatment of the child abuse scandals has shown that not only is the Catholic Church completely unsuited to this task but, worse than that, it has been the belief in the goodness of priests that has provided a cloak for many of the most terrible of acts.

Cardinal Seán Brady, Roman Catholic Archbishop of Armagh and Primate of All Ireland (Archbishop from 1996, Cardinal from 2007), has a history that demonstrates the moral bankruptcy of the Catholic Church on this matter.

In March 2010, Brady acknowledged that in his role as bishop's secretary in 1975, he had attended separate meetings where two victims of the paedophile priest Fr Brendan Smyth had been asked to sign an oath of silence as part of a church enquiry into claims against the priest.

The justification given for this oath was that it protected the integrity of the enquiry. What it did was to put the protection of the reputation of the Catholic Church above any due legal process and above the rights of the victims.

'I didn't have any decision-making power in it,' said Cardinal Brady. 'The reason for the oath was to give it credibility and strength in law and robustness against any challenge because he was going to use the evidence which this inquiry would produce to take disciplinary action. That inquiry got under way.'

'In the space of two or three weeks he had the firm reasons which he wanted to remove Father Brendan Smyth and he immediately set out to Kilnacrott Abbey (where Smyth was based) and did so. That's on the record.' (http://www.belfasttelegraph.co.uk/news/local-national/cardinal-sean-brady-i-didnt-help-hide-priests-child-abuse-28523575.html)

This claim does not stand up to scrutiny. For a start, the idea that Brady did not have a decision-making power is nonsense. He had the power to decide to report Smyth to the police. The locations of Smyth's crimes were such that he could have reported him either to the Northern Irish Police (The Royal Ulster Constabulary) or to the police in the Irish Republic (The Garda Síochána). Not only could Brady have reported Smyth but that is what he should have done. His failure exemplifies one of the greatest moral failings of religion: the belief that religion is more important than human beings. Brady is responsible for what he failed to do. His belief that he followed canon law does not remove that responsibility. It demonstrates how harmful it can be to put religious rules before the interests of people and, in this case, children. That failure had serious consequences; Smyth went on to offend again.

Yet in an interview with the Daily Mail on 15 March 2010, Brady claimed,

I did act, and act effectively, in that inquiry to produce the grounds for removing Father Smyth from ministry and specifically it was underlined that he was not to hear confessions and that was very important. (http://www.dailymail.co.uk/news/article-1257904/Irelands-Catholic-leader-Sean-Brady-paedophile-priest-cover-up.html#ixzz2VzYFeHp3)

The truth is more children were abused because Brady and other figures in the Catholic Church set loyalty to their church above that to any civil authority, and more importantly, they put that loyalty before the protection of children.

Smyth was not arrested until 1991 (sixteen years later) when he was charged with the abuse of four siblings on the Falls Road in Belfast. No one knows how many children he abused in the period between the 'inquiry' and his arrest. He skipped bail and went on the run ending up at Kilnacrott Abbey in County Cavan in the Irish Republic owned by the Norbertine religious order he was a member of.

The delays in his extradition to Northern Ireland led to the Irish Republic's Fianna Fail/Labour coalition government collapsing in 1994. It is to the credit of the then leader of the Irish Party Dick Spring that he forced the government to an end over the appointment of Harry Whelehan, the Attorney General (a political post), to a senior judicial post. Spring's concern was that the appointment put Whelehan beyond parliamentary scrutiny. An allegation was made by a member of the Dáil (Irish lower house) that the delay was due to the influence of the then Irish Primate Cardinal Cahal Daly. This was denied, and, to be fair, the accusation does not seem credible for one simple reason. The Catholic Church had no need to put pressure on the government.

The Irish Prime Minister (Taoiseach) Albert Reynolds was a Conservative Catholic, leading a Conservative Catholic political party. The 1937 constitution had enshrined the role of the Catholic Church and they had, and still largely have, a control of the school system. The reluctance of Harry Whelehan to extradite a priest to the largely Protestant Northern Ireland, and from Irish to British jurisdiction, was predictable but wholly lacking in principle. It put politics and specifically the protection of an Irish Catholic identity before justice and the protection of abused children. It became a critical factor, though not the only one, that led to the rift between the Catholic Church and a large part of the Irish population. Smyth was eventually imprisoned and died of a heart attack, shortly after commencing his sentence. Meanwhile, the story of child abuse continued to play out in Northern Ireland.

Throughout the long history of the Northern Irish 'Troubles', the East Belfast district of Ballyhackamore was largely, though not entirely, unaffected by the violence. The area had a certain kudos, as the childhood home of the author C.S. Lewis, and was immortalised in Van Morrison songs such as 'Cyprus Avenue' and 'Madame George'. There were a number of bombings and shootings, but it didn't go through the intense turmoil experienced in other parts of the city. Ballyhackamore was socially and religiously mixed. A large number of the residents were from the professional and business classes. While largely Protestant, it did have a sizeable Catholic minority who lived side by side with them on amiable terms.

In the mid-1970s, a new curate was appointed to the Catholic Church of St Colmcilles. Fr Joe Steele (Michael Joseph Steele) was in his mid-thirties and set about making an impact. He organised discos in the parochial hall and set up a gym club for young parishioners. This even attracted an involvement from a small number of non-Catholic kids.

Steele cultivated the image of the ideal priest. However, he had a very disturbing agenda. He inveigled his way into the hospitality of a family with adolescent

37

children, where he became a frequent dinner guest. We can only speculate that the family felt privileged that the young popular priest gave them so much of his time. But what we can say, with certainty, is they paid a very heavy price for their hospitality. In 1991, three, young adult, siblings accused Steele of abuse in front of his parishioners in his new parish in Newtownards. That must have taken great courage, and the victims had every right to expect the church to support their interests. Their concern was to prevent Steele from being allowed to work with children. They simply didn't want others to go through what they had gone through. The church failed them.

The bishop's immediate response was to order Steele to return to the headquarters of The Holy Ghost Order, of which he was a member. This was in Dublin, in the Irish Republic, and therefore outside the legal jurisdiction where he had committed the crimes. That Order at some point decided to export this paedophile to England. It is beyond comprehension how they could have thought that was OK. To simply send a paedophile as far away as they could, where more children would be vulnerable, was moral bankruptcy. There can be no justification for such a callous lack of concern for potential victims. Yet it is a pattern which is found in the case of paedophile priest after paedophile priest. It may not have been the official policy of the Catholic Church, but it looks like it was the de facto policy. It appears to have been implemented without informing either ecclesiastical or legal authorities at the receiving end as to why the priest was being exported.

Steele was eventually found five years later while working as a priest in the South Yorkshire town of Rotherham. He had been spotted by a sister of one of his victims. Once again, he returned to Dublin and, then no doubt persuaded by the knowledge of the Irish Government's extradition of Smyth, agreed to give himself up to the RUC.

In his first trial, it was shown that he had abused the girls regularly over a period of five years. In total, on that occasion, Steele pleaded guilty of sexually molesting two boys and three girls between the ages of nine and fifteen years of age.

In a later trial, he admitted to offences going back to 1967. He had committed many offences against both girls and boys. His sentencing on these charges was halted when he was declared dead from a brain tumour in January 2013. The question this raises is how did a priest with a largely affluent and well-educated congregation get away with this for so long?

I'm going to return to the subject of Joe Steele, but first, I'm going to address why priests, in Ireland, North and South, got away with abuse and then how their power has been challenged in recent years.

The desire for something that can be seen as special is very strong in humans. Religions exploit that desire. Most religions (there are a few exceptions such as the Quakers) create a special order of people or, in some cases, orders of people. They are the ordained and are usually treated with a degree of reverence. From Buddhist monks to the local evangelical pastor, this applies. One of the great dangers of religion is these people are given a special degree of trust and respect. They are seen as having a special knowledge and a direct route to the divine or whatever the revered idea at the heart of the religion is. They are assumed to be morally better than other people.

This is a symbiotic process because it is not just a case of the priest enjoying this status but also of the congregation reinforcing it. The shaman, the Indian mystic, the pastor, and priest all fulfil a desire to have a religious message conveyed by someone of a special status. In the Roman Catholic Church, there is belief in apostolic succession. Catholic ordination is claimed to have been derived in an unbroken line from the twelve apostles and therefore from Christ himself. This means the priest is the inheritor of a sacred legacy. He is seen as having the power to transform bread and wine into the body and blood of Christ. That alone makes a priest a very powerful figure. He is the keeper of a mystery.

The priest also has a high social status within the community. He is seen as a trusted professional like a doctor, lawyer, or teacher. Other professionals, within his religion, would see him as not just sharing that status but, because of his spiritual role, as have a pre-eminent status. That has meant a reluctance to question him because to do so would be to both question his spiritual and professional integrity.

I often tweet on the topics I am writing about. I get frequent abuse from believers. The level of abuse I've had from Catholics on this issue has been very high indeed. They seem to desperately want to bury the issue. However, one of the strongest voices against the abuse came from the Irish Prime Minister Enda Kenny, when, in July 2011, he attacked the Vatican over interference in an inquiry into clerical abuse of children in the diocese of Cloyne. Here are excerpts from his speech.

> Because for the first time in Ireland, a report into child sexual-abuse exposes an attempt by the Holy See, to frustrate an Inquiry in a sovereign, democratic republic . . . as little as three years ago, not three decades ago . . .

> Cloyne's revelations are heart-breaking. It describes how many victims continued to live in the small towns and parishes in which they were reared and in which they were abused . . . their abuser often still in the area and still held in high regard by their families and the community

> The abusers continued to officiate at family weddings and funerals . . . In one case, the abuser even officiated at the victim's own wedding . . .

> Cardinal Josef Ratzinger [Who by the time of the speech was Pope Benedict XVI] said: 'Standards of conduct appropriate to civil society or the workings of a democracy cannot be purely and simply applied to the Church.'

> As the Holy See prepares its considered response to the Cloyne Report, as Taoiseach, I am making it absolutely clear, that when it comes

to the protection of the children of this State, the standards of conduct which the Church deems appropriate to itself, cannot and will not, be applied to the workings of democracy and civil society in this republic.

Not purely, or simply or otherwise.

CHILDREN . . . FIRST. (http://www.rte.ie/news/2011/0720/303965-cloyne1/)

The Vatican's response was to deny that it had interfered in the inquiry. However, even if there was no direct interference from the Vatican, it is beyond question that elements within the church did seek to obstruct it. The simple truth is that again and again the Catholic Church has put its own interests first and only addressed the real harm when it has been forced to do so.

This story has played out across the globe. What happened in the Irish Catholic Church happened in the United States, Australia, South Africa, and many other places. The Catholic Church and other religions, including Buddhists, need to face up to the fact that the position of clergyman, minister, monk, and in some cases nun has been used for cruel forms of abuse.

Chapter Seven

EXPERIENCE

I knew Fr Joe Steele. I should say I was not a victim of his sexual abuse. Though I had not known what he had been doing at the time, when his trial was reported in the papers in 1996 (I had been living in England for many years by this time) I immediately knew who some of his victims had been. It had always been obvious that there was at least one family he was especially close to.

The parish was wealthy enough to provide a large house for each of its two priests. One was on the famous Cyprus Avenue (ironically in close proximity to the residence of the Rev. Ian Paisley). That occupied by Steele, who was the more junior priest, was a large semi-detached house, in the grounds of the church and the primary school. Yes, Fr Michael Joseph Steele, one of the most notorious of paedophile priests in the Irish Catholic Church, lived in the grounds of a primary school. My recollection, from something he had said, is he had chosen it rather than share the large Cyprus Avenue address with the other priest. It seems very clear that he had contrived a situation where he could be close to children and away from the gaze of his senior colleague.

It was to that house that, at the age of fifteen, I went to in distress on a wet night. My mother had died a couple of years before, and I couldn't cope with my father's manic depression. I needed an adult to talk to. I needed someone I felt I could trust.

I was one of the groups of teenage boys who used the weight training facilities Father Steele made available in his gym sessions. That was why he seemed a natural person to turn to in my distress. He had appeared to be understanding. I have no idea if he had any sexual interest in me, but it did later cross my mind that the fact he knew that the weight training had made me strong and physically confident may have deterred him. Steele may have ironically armed me against him.

41

Back in the 1970s, ideas such as emotional intelligence had no popular currency. Yet even then I had expected empathy. Instead of that expected understanding of why I was distressed over my father what I met from Steele was an astounding emotional blankness. At fifteen, I didn't have the words to explain such a complete absence of empathy. What I did understand was that he left me in no doubt that he had no interest in helping me.

Even at fifteen, I knew there was something wrong. Steele could play a part delivering his homilies, and, no doubt, he had a formula for confessions, but he had no comprehension as to how to deal with real human distress. The contrast between the public man and his apathetic response to me stunned me. It was the first time in my life I ever began to question the value of religion. In hindsight, it was extremely fortunate that it completely destroyed my confidence in Steele.

I was certainly no stranger to priests. I was taught by a number of them. The school I attended could not have been better connected to the Catholic hierarchy. The headmaster was Fr Joseph Conway, the brother of Cardinal William Conway. He basked in the formal title of 'President of the College', but I even recall one of his fellow priests calling him by his nick name, Joe Boss. The school was not very large, and he knew his pupils. I recall once being caned, on my palms, by him, for getting into a fight. I was struck by the irony of being violently punished for violence.

The school was in the parish of St Colmcilles. One of the priests who taught me often took services in the church. What he and the other priests who taught me knew about Steele I don't know. The idea that they would not have put the interests of the boys they taught, many of whom were potential victims of Steele, first, seems unthinkable. It may be that Steele fooled some very bright men, but I find it hard to escape the possibility that if a pupil had told the teachers at the school, of abuse by him, they simply wouldn't have believed it.

The school did nothing to control teachers who repeatedly practised corporal punishment. One Latin teacher (a lay teacher, as most were), whom we nicknamed 'The Weed', would stand beside us as we declined a verb and demand we held forth our palms, when we faltered. He'd raise his leather strap as high as he could and bring it down, with all the force he could muster, landing four sharp slaps, two on each hand. It caused stinging bright red marks, and we could do nothing but vigorously shake our hands to ease the terrible burning sensation. We considered ourselves fortunate if a number of others had been punished before us, as we knew the later swings of his strap carried less power.

This cruelty was justified by Proverbs 13: 24, which is often paraphrased as 'Spare the rod. Spoil the child.' It was, in fact, a remarkably stupid teaching strategy. If the approach had worked, it would have done so as a deterrent. A strapped boy would have shown improvement. I know of no evidence that it improved anyone's learning.

I was and still am moderately dyslexic. In adulthood, I've tried to learn the words of poem or song I have loved and have not been able to recall more than a line or two. I still can only rarely write a sentence without needing to correct it; if someone tells me their telephone number, I can't repeat it back to them. The numbers will jumble in my head, unless I slowly write them down.

My brain is agile when it comes to making connections, and I have no difficulty in grasping and countering an argument, but learning by rote is simply not a skill I possessed then or possess now. The ability to think was eventually to get me a place at university but was useless for remembering Latin declensions. I got strapped day after day, and year after year, for an inability that was not my fault.

It was punishment for the sake of punishment, and I cannot escape the perception that it was punishment for the joy of punishing. Those of us who were strapped at the beginning of the academic year were invariably still being strapped at the end of it. We were strapped for being lazy and stupid, but what could conceivably be more stupid than to have continued year after year to do something that had no result? All the beating in the world could not have given me the skills I did not have. How stupid and lazy is it to not question a teaching strategy that fails, fails, and fails again? It is hard to imagine how anyone could have had a more stupid and lazy approach to teaching than that of The Weed. He deserves to be addressed by no other name, than that. He used the strap as a substitute for intelligent teaching methods and didn't question its qualifications for the task. He showed no respect for the victims of his mindless cruelty.

While being regularly strapped had no effect on my learning, it did, however, have one important outcome; it beat every last trace of Roman Catholicism out of me. That is the only thing I thank The Weed for. When I was fifteen, this punishment eased off, and I began to question my treatment. The myth of a religion of love made no sense to me. It had been contradicted every time the strap had fallen. My anger at what had happened to me gradually grew. I abandoned the religion at the age of sixteen and have never wanted to call myself a Roman Catholic or be in any way associated with that church in the years since. That was, however, far from the end of my journey with religion and spirituality.

Even if I were not eventually to become an Atheist, a religion that treated me so cruelly would have forsaken any right to a claim on me. I more than once had the experience of a teacher who expounded on the theme of how loving and forgiving God was and yet could not grasp that beating me for my incapacity to learn by rote was cruel and the denial of every principle of love.

Jesus supposedly said, 'By their fruits do ye know them.' The fruits I found in Roman Catholicism were stupidity and cruelty. I do not mean by that that the school was poor academically. Far from it, in spite of the cruelty, it had some excellent teachers and excellent academic results.

It is an irony that one of the best of those teachers was a priest by the name of Fr John Forsythe. We called him Bruce after the television entertainer Bruce Forsyth. He protested there was a difference. He had an 'E' for excellence at the end of his name. He had not been long out of the seminary, when he taught us, and brought a keen understanding of textual criticism to his lessons. When I began later to dissect the Bible, my memories of his lessons gave me a good starting point.

I left the school as soon as I could and did my 'A' levels at a further education college. I do not call myself an ex-Catholic. I never joined Catholicism, but I left as soon as I was able to. It is not an institution I would have ever voluntarily joined or recommend to anyone else.

The Catholic Church presumes to teach morality yet had no comprehension of the harm it was doing. The futile vindictive punishments where bad enough but worse was the contempt they signified towards the pupils. That told boys so very clearly that they'd not be believed if they reported sexual abuse by a priest. That was not the intention of the school's brutal disciplinary regime, but what other outcome could there have been?

I have no reason to believe other than that John Forsythe was, and is, a decent and intelligent man. I hope he would have acted effectively had he been told of abuse by Steele. The problem is that religion demands that loyalty to it comes first. It claims sacred authority for that loyalty. The clergy are very dependent on it, especially where it provides not just their income but their housing. (I recall Forsythe stating that teaching priests are required to forego a high percentage of their income to the church.) The church could have brought great pressure to bear on a priest who made statements that were seen to damage its interests.

The Catholic Church wants to see child abuse by priests and nuns as simply an issue of some very bad priests and nuns. What it needs to understand is that the nature of religion compounded the problem. It allowed priests to have a status that placed them above suspicion. It fostered a myth that celibacy meant purity. It had schools that enforced authority by beating children and taught that authority figures should not be questioned. Men like Smyth and Steele will have understood the esteem in which priests were held and seen themselves as untouchable. They had every reason to, as the Catholic Church did a great deal to defend and enable them.

Chapter Eight

WOMAN IN THE BIBLE, QUR'AN, CHRISTIANITY, AND ISLAM

> Narrated by Ibn Abbas: The Prophet said: 'I was shown the Hell-Fire
> and that the majority of its dwellers were women who were ungrateful.'
> (Hadith 1.28)

The Hadith is a collection of eighth and ninth century writings on Muhammad and the Qur'an that form a guide to Islamic thinking. If you want to know what view the Qur'an (Koran) has of women, simply read the Surah (chapter) 4. It is entitled 'Women', and this is part of what it says:

> Men are in charge of women by [right of] what Allah has given one
> over the other and what they spend [for maintenance] from their wealth.
> So righteous women are devoutly obedient, guarding in [the husband's]
> absence what Allah would have them guard. But those [wives] from whom
> you fear arrogance—[first] advise them; [then if they persist], forsake them
> in bed; and [finally], strike them. But if they obey you [once more], seek no
> means against them. Indeed, Allah is ever Exalted and Grand. (Surah 4: 34)

There is argument over how firmly a man is entitled to strike his wife, but what is very clear is that this is not about an erotic game of playful and consensual spanking. This is about the fundamental denial of a woman's right to freedom. It is essentially stating that she is the property of her husband, whether she likes it or not. In Islam, this is defended on the basis that it defines the limits to which a man can go. In practice, it is often used as a justification for domestic violence.

The Qur'an is very precise about how men and women should be valued. When addressing the question of inheritance, it states:

Allah enjoins you concerning your children: for the male is the equal of the portion of two females; but if there be more than two females, two-thirds of what the deceased leaves is theirs; and if there be one, for her is the half. And as for his parents, for each of them is the sixth of what he leaves, if he has a child. (Surah 4: 11)

This is defended on the basis that it did give women defined inheritance rights, and that the Qur'an enshrined her rights, at a time when they were often denied property rights. That is not a justification for giving women in the twenty-first century medieval property rights. If the principle was to protect rights in a medieval contest, why are rights appropriate to modern times not protected? Not to do so turns a belief system, which by medieval standards was an enlightened one, in to a deeply oppressive one by modern standards.

The Qur'an makes it clear that a woman is only valued half as much as a man as a witness:

And call two witnesses from among your men, two witnesses. And if two men be not at hand, then a man and two women. (Surah 2: 282)

There are, of course, excuses, but these boil down to the attitude that women are less trustworthy than men. No excuse removes that attitude. The consequences of the rigid application of these attitudes have real effects today.

The information on the status of women originated from the Shadow Report for CEDAW prepared by 'Saudi Women for Reform', Saudi Arabia in December 2007. I was originally sent a copy of this report by a Saudi dissident who managed to get out of the country to pursue postgraduate study but was reported to the Saudi authorities for her Atheism, by her own family. The Saudi Government removed her funding, and she ended up having to seek asylum.

A copy of the final official report is available at http://olddoc.ishr.ch/hrm/tmb/treaty/cedaw/reports/cedaw%2040/cedaw_40_saudiarabia.pdf

It gives a more diplomatic assessment and couches cruelty in more polite terms than the victims do. However, even reading that you could be left in no doubt of the position of Saudi women. Here I have highlighted key points that can leave no one in any doubt as to how enslaved Saudi Women are. What follows is not my writing but the report. I have selected from it but not edited it.

While, since it was written, women have been given limited voting rights, in local elections, the position of women has not changed in any meaningful way. They remain in a position which is little better than imprisonment.

The original document is very worth reading. It is not a professional document but the authentic voice of those seeking freedom. It can be linked to at http://www2.ohchr.org/english/bodies/cedaw/docs/ngos/womenreform40.pdf

- Women are not allowed to enter all the government's departments including the administration of women's education and public institutions such as the Department of Social Insurance.
- Women are not allowed to enter many shops and shops classed as 'public service stores', such as video shops, music shops, children's barber shops, travel agencies, or foreign labour recruitment agencies.

This means women are often denied the right to use these resources or at risk of officials exploiting them if they seek them.

- Not allowed to issue an official document that combines the mother's identity information with her children's.

This denies women a legal recognition of parenthood, in many situations. The father is the parent for legal purposes.

- Not allowed to drive a car. Not allowed to ride any game while accompanying a child in a public place, such as a mall, or to ride in a boat in a public park.
- Not allowed into any sport clubs (all male), sport halls, or attend sport games, except with a mahram or guardian, or use the gym in a hotel outside of designated hours.

A mahram is a relative whom you can't marry like a father, mother, brother, or sister. Women are highly restricted in the activities they are allowed to take part in. This reflects a deep fear of female freedom.

- Not allowed to attend courses in schools, universities, postgraduate studies, except with permission from a guardian.
- Not allowed to travel abroad, except with a guardian's permission. If a woman does not have a guardian: a father or a husband or brother, then her son (even if he is very young) acts as her guardian.
- Not allowed to work without the permission of a guardian.
- Not allowed to stay in hotels, restaurants, café, or furnished flats without a mahram.

A woman basically can't do anything outside the home without male permission.

- Even in access to places of worship, women are discriminated against. They have limited access to mosques, being restricted in where and when they can pray.

A woman can't even make decision over her own health.

- A woman is not allowed to enter a hospital even for the birth of a child without a guardian's approval, nor she can be discharged from hospital or prison without a male guardian's signature.

She is not allowed to have an operation without the consent of a guardian, especially when it is a gynaecological operation.

- A woman in not allowed to register the birth of her own baby. Only the father or a male relative over seventeen years old can do so.
- A woman is not allowed to open a bank account in the name of her son or daughter except with the father's consent nor is she allowed to carry any out transactions on her child's behalf even if it is she who is depositing money in it.

The Qur'an was enlightened by medieval standards, but the reality is it is used in countries like Saudi Arabia to keep women in a medieval position today. Enlightened medieval standards are deeply oppressive in modern times. The justification is it protects women, but having rights protects people. Their denial leaves them at the mercy of the tyrannical. They are denied the most basic of human freedoms. In a free society, a woman should be entitled to dress as she chooses, including a burqa or a miniskirt. For her to be forced or pressurised into wearing either would be an infringement of her freedom. The simple fact is a burqa cannot protect a woman from rape, any more than a miniskirt can.

Strict dress codes do not make men respect women. On the contrary, they send out the message that women need to be controlled. That devalues women and hampers the healthy relationships between the sexes that allow for understanding. At heart, the arguments against women dressing, as they wish, come down to a deep fear of female sexuality and the desire to control and contain it. That theme runs through much of religion, even where a modest dress code is no longer imposed.

It is there in the Garden of Eden story—the idea that a woman is easily tempted and will lead men astray. It gives men an excuse not to look at their own sexuality, with honesty and maturity. Human sexuality can be complex, and religion often offers myths like if women didn't look sexy, men wouldn't have desires. That can lead to the second and more dangerous myth that a man's actions are the fault of the woman he desires.

How does it protect a woman if she can't decide her own course of study at university? Why is it assumed that a woman is less able to enter into a legal contract than a man? Why should a capable woman be required to have any form of guardianship or supervision she does not want? Why is a woman any more at risk than a man when she drives a car?

There is nothing in this supposed protection of a woman that could not be simply be just as easily termed as domination of her. No society can be said to respect human rights if it does not let a woman walk away from such domination and protect her right to decide on how she dresses, is educated, enters contracts, travels, and lives her life.

It is a common mistake to assume that calls for the harsh treatment of women are confined to the Qur'an. As we will see, the Bible orders women to be treated in horrendous ways that match and even exceed the cruelty of the Qur'an. If fundamentalist Jews and Christians wish to proclaim the Bible as the source of religious authority or the inerrant the word of God, they need to face up to what it says about the treatment of women.

In the Qur'an, we find:

> And as for those of your women who are guilty of an indecency, call to witness against them four (witnesses) from among you; so if they bear witness, confine them to the houses until death takes them away or Allah opens a way for them.
> And as for the two of you who are guilty of it, give them both a slight punishment; then if they repent and amend, turn aside from them. Surely Allah is ever Oft-returning (to mercy), the Merciful. (Surah 4: 15-16)

The first verse refers to a woman who misbehaves sexually. The second refers to men. The inequality is striking. Women are imprisoned for life for sexual misconduct. That's a very severe punishment indeed. Men can be forgiven if they repent. The attitude is it is only natural for men to misbehave, but if a woman does so, she is a whore, who should be locked up.

Severe as this is, it does compare to a biblical remedy for some women who seek to exercise sexual freedom.

> And the daughter of any priest, if she profane herself by playing the whore, she profaneth her father: she shall be burnt with fire. (Lev. 21: 9)

Yes, this is a God of compassion. If you are a priest and your daughter starts to sleep around, it is your duty to have her burnt. This is so horrific that we'd hope it was a mistranslation, but if we go to the complete Jewish Bible, we find:

> If a kohen's [Priest's] daughter becomes desecrated through adultery she desecrates her father; she shall be burned in fire. (Vayikra—Lev. 21:9)

Of course, we might think these words come from one of those ranting prophets in the Bible that no one takes any notice of. Well, the answer to that is we are very clear whom both the Torah and Bible attribute these remarks to; it is to one of the most important figures in Judaism, Christianity, and Islam: Moses.

No mention is made of the man who sleeps with her unless, of course, she is married. Then it is adultery. It is important to understand that adultery, in this period, was sleeping with another man's wife and not sleeping with a concubine or slave girl.

There is an argument that this horrifying punishment only applies to a married daughter. The puzzling thing about that is, why would her father, rather than her husband, have been relevant? And odder still is the question of why that would make any difference to the horror of the situation? Whether she was a teenager or more mature woman makes no difference to the horror of a woman being burnt to death.

The answer to why there is such punishment for the daughter of a priest lies in a topic I doubt is often the theme of sermons and I'm certain isn't mentioned in Sunday school: temple prostitutes. We know that this was a persistent issue because of the repeated condemnations of it.

> Thou shalt not bring the hire of a whore, or the price of a dog,
> into the house of the Lord thy God for any vow: for even both these are
> abomination unto the Lord thy God. (Deut. 23: 18)

It is worth noting that the condemnation is not of prostitutes per se but of the sacred prostitute. The term 'dog' appears to refer to male prostitutes. The use of temple prostitutes was linked to idolatry. The control of sexual activity, the stamping out of it as an integral part of worship, was inseparable from seeking religious compliance. This, of course, links back to the desire to control marriage within the Books of Ezra and Nehemiah and hatred that evoked. It is also reflected in Israel straying from the true faith, meaning she is compared to a harlot.

> For of old time I have broken thy yoke, and burst thy bands; and thou
> sadist, I will not transgress; when upon every high hill and under every
> green tree thou wanderest, playing the harlot. (Jer. 2: 20)

This symbolism is repeated again and again. To not conform religiously and to misbehave sexually are equated. This put an interesting complexion on the story of the woman taken in adultery in John 8: 3-11. It is one of the best known gospel stories. Like everything else in the gospels, its origins cannot be verified. But essentially the story goes that the scribes and Pharisees bring Jesus a woman, who has been caught in the very act of adultery, and point out that the Law of Moses states she should be stoned to death. Jesus says, 'Let whichever of you is without sin cast the first stone.' He then proceeds to draw on the ground with a stick and all of them, supposedly realising their sinful nature, drift away.

We could start by wondering why, if the Pharisees and scribes saw themselves as the religious authorities, they'd want to consult Jesus, on the matter. That aside, we need to question the role this story plays. Jews, at the time it was written, would have understood the symbolism of the prostitute in religious proclamations and discourse. Those who breached religious conformity were compared to a fallen woman. Jesus was being accused of breaching religious conformity. The story is an attempt to demonstrate that Jesus has overturned the authority of the Pharisees and scribes. He now dictates what religious conformity is. This is the point of the story, and it is not Jesus saying men and women should be treated equally. We don't need to look far to see that.

> Wives, submit yourselves unto your own husbands, as unto the
> Lord. For the husband is the head of the wife, even as Christ is the head
> of the church: and he is the saviour of the body. Therefore as the church
> is subject unto Christ, so let the wives be to their own husbands in every
> thing. (Eph. 5: 22-24)

The New Testament has no message of female emancipation. It treats women as either saints or whores. Mary, the mother of Jesus, is the perfect woman, submissive to God and her husband. The next most prominent woman is Mary Magdalene, who is recorded as being one of the first persons to have seen the risen Christ. That must have seemed to be too prominent a role for a woman, as Christianity was developed in later centuries. Those who shaped the story of the resurrection found a way to diminish the importance of Mary Magdalene. Without anything in the gospels, to justify their claim, they compounded her story with that of the adulterous woman whom Jesus saved. So for centuries, Mary Magdalene was the whore Jesus had saved. There were alternative gospels that gave her a more prominent role than in the New Testament. They were rejected.

When the author of the Revelation of John, the last apocalyptic book of the Bible, sought a term to describe the source of all evil, it is no accident that he lit upon the term 'Whore of Babylon'. 'Whore' was the worst insult he could conjure up and that link with Babylon brings us back again to the Books of Ezra and Nehemiah.

> And the woman was arrayed in purple and scarlet colour, and decked
> with gold and precious stones and pearls, having a golden cup in her hand full
> of abominations and filthiness of her fornication: And upon her forehead was
> a name written, MYSTERY, BABYLON THE GREAT, THE MOTHER OF
> HARLOTS AND ABOMINATIONS OF THE EARTH. (Rev. 17: 4-5)

The most evil image he could conjure up was what we might call today a liberated and sexually active woman. How can anyone find a message of female emancipation in that? But let's face it the Bible isn't very big on emancipation. In fact, it encourages the opposite.

Chapter Nine

SLAVERY

'The thing you have to understand about slavery back then, in biblical times, is it wasn't like slavery the way we think of it today. It wasn't cruel. It was just like having a job.' This is what many Christians have been told by teachers, priests, or pastors. They may have emphasised that translations of the Bible used the words such as 'servant', 'manservant', or 'bondservant' rather than slave. They might have tried to convince you that slavery, in the Bible, was no worse than the treatment of servants in TV costume dramas such as Downton Abbey.

Well, if you have been told that, or something similar, by someone who claims to have studied what the Bible says on this matter, there is no delicate way to put this: you have been lied to. That is not something I say lightly. However, either the person, who spun you this line, lied about what the Bible says, or they lied about having read it. There is no justification for such claims in the Bible. Such claims are excuses for appalling cruelty.

> When a man sells his daughter as a slave, she shall not go out as the male slaves do. If she does not please her master, who has designated her for himself, then he shall let her be redeemed. He shall have no right to sell her to a foreign people, since he has broken faith with her. If he designates her for his son, he shall deal with her as with a daughter. If he takes another wife to himself, he shall not diminish her food, her clothing, or her marital rights. And if he does not do these three things for her, she shall go out for nothing, without payment of money. (Exod. 21: 7-11, English Standard Version (ESV))

Now what, exactly, do you think is going on in this passage? It starts with 'When a man sells his daughter.' It doesn't say that 'a man selling his daughter is indescribably evil'. No. It is OK for a man to sell his daughter; the normal sort of thing any dad would do. How many sermons have your heard starting with those words? But there they are in the Bible.

Well, you will hear the claim that the young woman referred to, in the passage above, is protected because she can't be sold to foreigners. Not much of a protection when she can be given to her master's son and treated as a spare wife. Her consent to this is notably absent from the text. So let us be clear about what this passage says. A young woman can be sold to another man, by her father, then given to his son, who can marry her, but when he wants another woman, he can treat her as a spare wife. So long as she is fed and clothed properly and given her marital rights, she has no say in the matter. Marital rights in theory protect her from being sexually forced. However, the Bible stipulates no punishment for marital rape, and even in the case of a single woman, the fifty shekels of silver fine is paid to her father, and she'll be given to the rapist in marriage (see 'The Problem of Evil' later).

What are we non-believers making a fuss about? Surely, anybody can see that is just a normal employment contract? The supposedly generous employment rights only apply to Hebrew slaves. The Bible makes it very clear that foreigners who are enslaved aren't entitled to even meagre rights.

> As for your male and female slaves whom you may have: you may buy male and female slaves from among the nations that are around you. You may also buy from among the strangers who sojourn with you and their clans that are with you, who have been born in your land, and they may be your property. You may bequeath them to your sons after you to inherit as a possession forever. You may make slaves of them, but over your brothers the people of Israel you shall not rule, over one another ruthlessly. (Lev. 25: 44-46, ESV)

Once again, that is just like a normal employment contract. Most employment contracts state that you are our employers property and so are your children and so are theirs forever. Slavery in the Old Testament meant slavery. It is a lie to say otherwise. There is, of course, an aspect of Hebrew law that those who defend slavery in the Bible like to refer to.

> Now these are the rules that you shall set before them. When you buy a Hebrew slave, he shall serve six years, and in the seventh he shall go out free, for nothing. (Exod. 21: 1-2, ESV)

Now that almost looks like no more than a fixed-term employment contract. But this is a passage which is often dishonestly quoted out of context. Let's just see what the rest of the contract says:

> If he comes in single, he shall go out single; if he comes in married, then his wife shall go out with him. If his master gives him a wife and she bears him sons or daughters, the wife and her children shall be her master's, and he shall go out alone. But if the slave plainly says, 'I love my master, my wife, and my children; I will not go out free,' then his master shall bring him to God, and he shall bring him to the door or the doorpost. And his master shall bore his ear through with an awl, and he shall be his slave forever. (Exod. 21: 3-6)

So if a slave is given a wife by his master, she and any children remain the property of the master. The only way the slave can stay with them is to agree to be a slave forever.

Apologists for Bible slavery will point out a master couldn't just kill his slaves. That was forbidden. The amount of cruelty that was allowed was set out:

> When a man strikes his slave, male or female, with a rod and the slave dies under his hand, he shall be avenged. But if the slave survives a day or two, he is not to be avenged, for the slave is his money. (Exod. 21:20-21)

So if a slave was beaten and lay in agony for a couple of days, before dying, that was OK. Serious violence against a slave was permitted.

I often hear the argument that while there was slavery in the Old Testament, Jesus didn't believe in slavery. When in March 2012 American Atheists in Pennsylvanian put up a poster quoting Colossians 3: 22 'Slaves Obey Your Master' with the image of an African slave, with his neck shackled, there was outrage at the image. Those outraged did not direct their anger at the Bible, which was the source of the verse, but at those who pointed out what the Bible says. They were reluctant to believe that the Bible endorses slavery, and many were even convinced that it condemned it in the New Testament. They were simply wrong. The New Testament tells slaves to obey their masters three times.

> Slaves, obey your earthly masters in everything; and do it, not only when their eye is on you and to win their favour, but with sincerity of heart and reverence for the Lord. (Col. 3: 22)
>
> Slaves, submit yourselves to your masters with all respect, not only to those who are good and considerate, but also to those who are harsh. (Pet. 2:18)
>
> Slaves, obey your earthly masters with respect and fear, and with sincerity of heart, just as you would obey Christ. (Eph. 6:5)

In Roman times, slaves often did the work of household servants, but they still had the legal status of slaves and were bought, sold, and treated with no more significance than livestock. Slaves, and in particular female slaves and boys, in the Roman world could be often forced into prostitution.

> Most prostitutes in imperial Rome were slaves who had been sold into the industry, thus accentuating their status as a commodity unable to act in their own interests. (E. Fenton, 'Prostitution as Labor in Imperial Rome', Studies in Mediterranean Antiquity and Classics, Vol. 1, Imperial Women, Iss. 1, Article 3)

Changing the term slave to servant in many translations does not change the status that slaves endured in biblical times. It does not change a history where slaves were sexually abused. There should be no doubt but that to defend slavery in Roman times is to defend forced prostitution and paedophilia.

This was not something the earliest Christians opposed.

> Christians who are slaves should give their masters full respect so that the name of God and his teaching will not be shamed. If your master is a Christian, that is no excuse for being disrespectful. You should work all the harder because you are helping another believer by your efforts. Teach these truths, Timothy, and encourage everyone to obey them. (1 Tim. 6: 1-2, New Living Translation)

So it is beyond question that both the Old and New Testaments supported slavery. All the excuses in the world will not make that fact go away. The verses above were used for centuries to justify slavery. Slave owners declared that the institution of slavery was ordained by God. They didn't find it hard to find Bible verses to support that assertion. That it does not sit well with the idea of Christianity, as a religion of love, leaves a serious question over the claims that Christianity is a religion of love. That might be uncomfortable, for Christians, but that doesn't make it untrue. Both the Old and New Testaments had authors who supported the institution of slavery. That is the reality.

The Bible has, throughout history, been used to justify slavery. It was used to justify apartheid in South Africa. To address such cruelty has never been religion's first priority. Throughout history, religions have all looked at the spiritual journey as more important than the immediate needs or rights of humanity.

While there have been those like Martin Luther King and Desmond Tutu who have harnessed religion to a struggle for human liberty, throughout the vast majority of history religion has had a message that the poor and oppressed should accept their lot. In fact, in both the US southern states and South Africa, far from opposing apartheid, many of the churches had been segregated between black and white. They were active participants in the injustice that suppressed the rights of non-whites. Up until the 1960s, many churches in the US southern states maintained a 'whites only' policy.

> 'Racism has lived like a malignancy in the bone marrow of this church for years,' said Bishop William Boyd Grove, the ecumenical officer for the church's Council of Bishops. 'It is high time to say we're sorry.'
> (Speaking in 2000, http://www.beliefnet.com/News/2000/05/Methodists-Issue-Sweeping-Apology-For-Churchs-Racism.aspx#)

It is worth noting that a tradition of Christianity that once, with such certainty, preached the separation of the races now preaches the separation of humanity from evolutionary history. So now that they can no longer declare superiority over other humans, they still determinately do it with respect to other animals. There is an argument that Creationism arose as transference of racist feelings to a more acceptable topic. The irony is these claims are often now accepted by those who were once victims of that racism. We will address evolution later, but for now it is time to ask how we know what is true.

Chapter Ten

How Do We Decide What s True?

This book has a number of themes, but one of them is the simple question: how do we know what is true? We live in a world with competing claims and many assertions of truth, and this can lead to the idea that truth is merely a subjective concept. This claim suits the approach of most religions and allows them to confuse the ideas of truth and belief. They also divorce the term 'truth' from that which can be objectively shown to be true. They try to turn truth into a matter of belief. But that does not stop subjective facts from being true. What matters about gravity is that it exists. Having the perception that it didn't would have no effect on that. It is worth starting by understanding how the confusion that separates truth from what is true starts.

For most of us, knowledge of the world starts from the perceptions of our senses and the authority of others. In infancy, we decide if a food is nasty or nice on the basis of our taste buds. Cabbage being horrible, but ice cream being nice, becomes part of our internalised knowledge system. Knowledge through the senses remains our most essential form of knowledge, and we'd not get very far without it. It is our most immediate and constant form of interaction with the world. However, neither the statement that cabbage tastes nasty or ice cream tastes nice is an objective truth. The senses are not always a very reliable guide to what is true.

It is our brain, and not our eyes, that creates our image of the world. And I only need to remove my glasses for a good deal of the world's detail to disappear. Furthermore, what my senses tell me might be very different from yours. In the unlikely, but not impossible, event that you were a child who liked cabbage but hated ice cream, you will be a shining example of my point. Our senses are subjective. Our sight, sense of smell, taste, hearing, and the sensitivity of our touch are all particular to us. They are a large part of what forms our perception of the world. Critically, perception is at the heart of religion, and it is the parent of much of religious belief.

Religions rely, in some circumstances, on the perception of the individual and more widely on trusting the perceptions of others. In many cases, a high value is often placed on the reliability of the perceptions of religious figures who are believed to have lived in the past. In the case of Mormonism that is within recent centuries. With Scientology, it is within the lifetime of many people still alive today. However, in each case, faith depends on accepting the perceptions of another person and a conviction that an often distant figure had profound insights.

This faith is often confirmed by the individual interpreting through their personal experience. A brilliant sunset may be seen as evidence of a benevolent God, who created a beautiful world. Such confirmation is often highly selective. Only factors that are seen to support the belief are identified as evidence. Any contrary evidence is ignored. A tsunami is not seen as evidence of the wonder of God. Yet it is as much a natural event as a fine sunset. The acceptance of a claim of perception, and the assertion that it is evidence of divine authority, is often central to the claims of a religion.

Muslims rely on the claim that when Muhammad spent time fasting in his cave, his perception that he was visited by the Angel Gabriel, who dictated the Qur'an to him, was correct. Christians rely on their perception that accounts of the gospels, with their claims about the miracles of Jesus, virgin birth, resurrection, and so on, are true. Buddhists rely on the perception of the Buddha that he had reached an enlightened state. In each of these cases, the perception is re-enforced by a belief in those who still today proclaim the accounts to be true.

As we grow, we acquire a wider knowledge of the world from parents, siblings, and other children. Later, those who teach us also become arbiters of our truth. What we see as true comes from the authority we invest in these people, and we quickly learn to see truth as competitive. We are apt to decide that what our friends tell us is true, and when those we dislike tell us the opposite, it is untrue. So our way of deciding what is true becomes based on accepting the authority of those we love and respect and prejudice against those we dislike.

Of greater force than the influence of our friends is that of our parents. What they say is true, and if someone has been told something different by their parents, we conclude that they must be wrong. This gives a tremendous emotional power to what we see as true. It is important to see how much of our initial understanding of what is true was formed through our senses and emotions.

That emotional attachment often appears to be what people define as faith. I often find in discussions with believers that they put great store on the claim that an authority figure has made about truth.

In some cases, a holy book such as the Bible or the Qur'an is used as a surrogate authority figure, but the principle is the same. 'It is true because my mummy, the Bible, or the Qur'an says so.' This attitude is starkly expressed in the words of one of Creationism's greatest apologists.

> When science and the Bible differ, science has obviously misinterpreted its data. (Henry M. Morris, Cofounder of Creationist Science)

There can never be intellectual honesty, in this approach, as it allows for the dismissal of any argument that doesn't fit a belief on no other basis than belief. Each religion, and often denomination, or sect within a religion, asserts that truth lies in their belief. Yet if this approach defines truth in one religion, why should it not apply to all belief systems? It has, for many, had the effect of making all understandings of the world relative to belief systems rather than testable to objective measureable facts. It comes down to no more than, if I believe something it must be true, and my belief is true because I believe it.

We say something is true because we were brought up to believe it, but how can we say that is a basis to assert an objective truth? We'd face the problem that other people will have been brought up to believe something else, and will have precisely the same justification, for what they believe. What we were brought up to believe was simply an accident of birth. If we followed the logic of that decision, we'd end up with no means to decide on objective truth and a dependence on authority figures for everything. That, of course, is an extreme scenario, but the point is dependency on a belief or an authority figure may give us a means to decide what to believe, but it gives us no methodology to test the truth of our beliefs. There is, however, an alternative approach.

One of the most essential differences between the approach of religion and that of science or history, to knowledge, is found in the role of authority figures. It is not that there is no respect for leading scientific figures. However, they are not authorities who decide what is true.

When, in 1953, James Watson and Francis Crick discovered DNA, their personal authority had nothing to do with it. DNA does not exist because we have faith in what they said or faith in them. Scientists accepted what Watson and Crick had said because they checked and double-checked it and looked at every possible way, in which, it could be wrong. There were men who had a very strong interest in doing so.

Linus Pauling, who was to win two noble prizes himself, was working on DNA at the same time. If Crick and Watson had been wrong, he would have wasted no time in telling the scientific community of their errors. It was the evidence that Linus Pauling, and the rest of the world, had to accept.

Authority does not make a scientific claim true. It does not matter how distinguished a scientist is; evidence is the currency of science. That does not mean that scientists don't argue over the interpretation, relevance of evidence, or the use of it. They do. The point is that evidence is the only reliable way to understand the nature of the material world, and the greatest discovery in the world is not a discovery until there is evidence it has been discovered.

Even if they'd no rivals, Watson and Crick's claims, about DNA, would have needed to be published in a peer-reviewed scientific journal, to be recognised. A 'peer-reviewed' article means that the article needs to have been scrutinised by other experts in the field before it is published. That means it can't just be something that is thought or believed to be true; the reasons why it is true must be clearly presented and checkable by others in the field. How that criterion is met will, of course, differ from discipline to discipline.

This means something very important: if a scientific claim is recognised, you can trace back the reasons why it is. You may need to do a demanding course of study to understand it, but the reasoning behind it can be traced back. It can be traced back through earlier experiments and to the earlier discoveries in the field.

> There is not a discovery in science, however revolutionary, however sparkling with insight, that does not arise out of what went before. 'If I have seen further than other men' said Isaac Newton, 'it is because I have stood on the shoulders of giants.' (Isaac Asimov in Adding a Dimension: Seventeen Essays on the History of Science (1964))

Knowledge piles upon knowledge, and even the most brilliant idea is dependent on previous knowledge. One of the myths about this approach is that scientific understandings based on double-blind experiments and a great deal of repetition is the only evidence supposedly 'hard core' Atheists like Richard Dawkins and godless scribblers like me accept. That is wrong.

The scientific method is the best way to test a claim, for which evidence is not readily available and where the conclusion is open to question. If you are reading this in, for instance, London or New York, the evidence of where you are does not need to be peer-reviewed in a scientific journal, before it is established. There will be many forms of evidence that can show that the city you are in is the one you say. If the evidence for the existence of God was as good as that which can be shown for London being London or New York being New York, then God would be an established fact. The point is that no such evidence exists. No verifiable evidence, of any kind, exists. Another source of evidence is historical evidence.

While the study of history allows for more latitude over interpretation than science, the same essential principle applies. You cannot construct an historical argument without evidence. The most common form of historical evidence is documentary evidence, but physical evidence from sources such as archaeological finds or the landscape can be just as important. Good history is about using all the available evidence to create as accurate picture and clear understanding of the past as is possible.

Religions regard themselves as having a form of diplomatic immunity from the standards of evidence applied in history or science. They claim that their understanding comes from a higher source than the human intellect. The problem with this is that there is no evidence that any of their holy books or the other claims of religion come from anywhere beyond the human intellect. This raises the question of why do we need to hold religion to as high a standard of evidence as science or history? Why does it matter?

Richard Dawkins writing about fundamentalist Christians in The God Delusion (2006) says:

> The truth of the holy book is an axiom, not the end product of a process of reasoning. The book is true, and if the evidence seems to contradict it, it is the evidence that should be thrown out.

As Dawkins points out, religion will always protect its central claims irrespective of the facts. Now it is true that over time religions have accepted many scientific claims, but they have always done that on their own terms. Some of these changes in understanding have been widely accepted, and others remain a matter of hot dispute.

One that is now widely accepted is that Earth is not, as was once claimed, the centre of the universe. However, most theistic religions still claim the universe was willed by God. They proclaim that the existence of the universe is evidence of the wonder and glory of God. What they have done here is alter their definition of what God does but continue to assert his creative role.

First, these religions claimed that God created the Earth at the centre of the universe, with the sun and planets rotating around it. Then Copernicus challenged that viewpoint. The initial reaction of the Catholic Church was to reject the claim. The Congregation of the Index (the Vatican's censorship committee) decreed on 5 March 1616 that the work by Copernicus that expounded this theory in his work De revolutionibus orbium coelestium (On the Revolutions of the Celestial Spheres) was forbidden 'until corrected'. It sounds like a student essay, with a few typing errors, that a pedantic professor has returned. They were, in fact, the nine sentences which defined the work, the ones that proclaimed that the heliocentric system (the Earth going round the Sun) was a certainty. It took until 1620 before this august body even got round to telling Copernicus which corrections they required. Left with no other option, he agreed to the changes. This done, the reading of the book was allowed. In other words, the book could be published, so long as the most important parts of it were omitted.

It was in 1632 that the controversy erupted, with a publication by Galileo which discussed Copernicus's heliocentrism. This led, in the following year, to the famous Galileo Trial where he was convicted after the intervention of the Pope, who refused to simply let him recant his 'error'. He was convicted of 'vehement suspicion of heresy' (Revolutionaries of the Cosmos, I.S. Glass, Oxford University Press, 2006, p. 33). This basically meant they couldn't actually prove he was a heretic, but the suspicion was grave enough for sanctions to be imposed against him. His crime had not been that he believed that the Earth went round the Sun but that he expressed that view publically. To be fair, his treatment was lenient, by the standards of the time. The verdict had much more to do with asserting the authority of the Catholic Church than seeking to brand Galileo a heretic. As we know, the Catholic Church eventually accepted what it had been very suspicious of. What had once been a profound truth simply slipped away.

This raises a very important question for any religious believer reading this book: which is more important, a belief or the truth? This question obviously applies to evolution, which we address later. It also applies to a number of other questions.

If you are a Christian, it equally applies to questions such as: Did the virgin birth happen? What about the miracles and the resurrection of Jesus? The question is not did these events actually happen, as stated, but is it more important that you believe in them or is it more important that the claims are true? The same question applies to Muslims. Is what you believe about how the Qur'an was written, or the truth about the origins of it, more important?

A discussion of the evidence of some of these claims will be addressed later. But to be clear, the questions are (a) do you believe in any of these claims? and (b) are these claims true? These are two separate and different questions. Assuming you do believe in one or more of these claims, I'm asking you to question if your belief or the truth of the claim is more important. I have laboured this point because it isn't one you are likely to have been asked in your church or mosque. You may well have never been encouraged to consider the distinction between these two questions before.

The problem is that most religions don't put the stress on the importance of establishing what is true but simply expect their claims to be believed. Belief, and not what is true, is their central concern. If you say that what you believe is true, simply on the basis that you believe it, you are setting up your belief as the arbiter of truth. Even if you argue that the arbiter of that truth is not you but the guidance of a holy book, church, or spiritual guide, it is you who are deciding that is where truth lies. It is your decision to accept that authority, though the acceptance may have been, and in most cases was, originally made on your behalf. It is important to understand that if something is accepted as true simply on the basis of faith, that faith will act as a barrier to honestly assessing the truth of it.

If, however, seeking the truth is put before faith, we could start by questioning the reliability of the sources of authority. Robin Lane Fox (The Unauthorized Version, 1991), as part of a very good examination of the Bible's merits as an historical source, explains the approach to evidence taken by the authors of the Old Testament.

> Among the Jews, the biblical authors inherited old and anonymous
> books about very remote times, but their existence was a barrier to
> critical method and doubt; they wrote unreservedly about events where

there was no primary knowledge. Good history, with a method, was born
not from this type of work but from personal interview and inquiry. (The
Unauthorized Version, 1991)

The point Prof. Lane Fox makes is that the Bible was not written as an accurate
historical account. Old Testament authors wrote it to preserve a belief. He later
illustrates how New Testament authors wrote the books in it as a means of spreading
a new one. He compares the writing of the Bible to works of the ancient Greek
historian Herodotus. In modern terms, Herodotus would be seen as taking great
liberties with the text. He makes up speeches. But the difference was Herodotus took
liberties in order to convey as full as possible an account of what, to the best of his
knowledge, had actually happened. The Bible authors subjugated historical truth to
their need to present their belief. In other words, the stories in the Bible were selected
and told in a manner that fitted the belief, and not the truth of what had happened.

The problem is simply this, we either say the history of the world is an account
of what has actually happened in it, or we say it is an account of what fits a belief
system. If a belief system is the guide, those who promote it will only allow events
which fit with their belief to be part of their account. In the case of the Bible, they
even inserted accounts of events, like the exodus, for which no verifiable historical
account or archaeological evidence has ever been found.

If we accept this approach, as valid, we might as well forget any search for truth
in the world, if it conflicts with a belief system. This is not just the position of those
who reject evolution; it goes to the heart of the claims of all the major religions.
They treat claims that are at best mythological, and in many cases outright fiction, as
profound truths. They say truth is the first casualty of war. It is, undoubtedly, also the
first casualty of any account of history written from a religious perspective.

I accept that when it comes to the degree they will accept evidence, believers
differ greatly. Most moderate Christians now accept the Theory of Evolution and
the idea of the Big Bang. These moderate believers have found an easy way to
accommodate this scientific discovery within their belief system. They say that God
caused the Big Bang.

In April 2013, I had the opportunity to ask Martin Rees (Baron Rees of Ludlow),
the Astronomer Royal, about this phenomenon. I said, 'So we don't know what
happened before the Big Bang?'

He said, 'About thirty or forty years ago, we weren't sure about the Big Bang.
So in thirty or forty years time, we might well know what was before the Big Bang.'
If that is what happens, the explanation that God was behind the Big Bang will have
to be reassessed by moderate Christians. His role in the creation of the world may be
seen as much further back in the past. He is already a God whose explanation has
been repeatedly redefined by scientific discoveries, but if he slips into the infinite
past, it is going to be very hard to explain his creative role. For all this believers have
still got one argument they cling to.

The Absence of Evidence Is Not Evidence of Absence of Argument

The argument goes: look at all the things that have been discovered over time, that no one believed could exist, before they were discovered. We non-believers are accused of being like those who dismissed any possibility of humans taking to the air in flight. Just because there is no evidence for something, doesn't mean it isn't true, we are told. That is true. However, it is a very poor argument for believing something there is no evidence for to be true. Let's consider why.

Let's take a hypothetical situation where we accept a belief, for which there is no evidence, and the next day someone presents us with an opposing belief, which is also without evidence. We'd be faced with a dilemma. Should we stick with the first belief or go with the second? How are to decide between the two claims when we have no evidence for either? We could toss a coin, but that would seem very arbitrary. This raises an important question. Is there any way of deciding between two claims, which are without evidence, which is any less arbitrary than tossing a coin?

Let's start with a well-known way of answering a question on some TV shows: we could phone a friend. We could do that, but, if there is no evidence for either belief, how is our friend any more qualified to answer the question than we are? It is not as though they might know the answer. If there is no evidence for something, we can't convey knowledge of it, because the conveying of knowledge would be evidence. All our friends could do would be to give us an opinion, and that could only be a guess, and therefore, no answer. So in this situation, our friend wouldn't be of any use, and we'd need another approach.

We could decide to stick with our first belief because then we would look like we were being consistent. However, while appearing to be consistent is an extremely common approach, it is no way to decide what is true.

Another approach would be to follow the option our parents and grandparents chose. This might feel like the most loyal option, but it does not tell us what is true. Even if they tell us which option we should decide on, and insist that it is what our family has always done for generations, that does not make that option true. This is another important point. A parent or other authority figure telling us to follow a belief, which is without evidence, does not make it true. They may have believed it, but they didn't know it was true.

Religions claim to have truth at their heart, but their core beliefs are all without evidence, and essentially arbitrary. There is no evidence for God, and there is no argument for belief in him (or her in the case of Goddesses like Gaia), which is any less arbitrary than the points we have just been through. I should, at this point say that this includes, not just say about the theistic religions but also Buddhism where belief in nirvana, the enlightenment story of the Buddha, or selection of a Dalai Lama are also a matter of belief.

Those who believe in a God usually do so on the grounds of faith. Religions are structured to reinforce that belief. They use powerful human sentiments to do so. One example is the power of families in maintaining adherence to the faith. J. Anderson Thomson, Jr., writing with Clare Aukofer argues that family relationships are very important in forming religious beliefs.

> Religions evoke and exploit kin emotions. Roman Catholicism offers a superb example. The nuns are 'sisters' or even 'Mother Superiors', the priests are 'Fathers', the monks are 'brothers' the Pope is the 'Holy Father' and the religion itself is referred to as the 'Holy Mother Church'. (Why We Believe in God(s), 2001)

This doesn't just apply to the Catholic Church. Smaller churches do the same thing. They act like an extended family. The idea of the pastor tending his flock is deeply paternalistic. The rabbi and imam perform similar roles.

What those of us brought up in a religious faith were told was true, was reinforced by God having a special day and by needing to attend a church, a mosque, a synagogue, or temple. Everything we saw and heard in those buildings, the symbols, such as crosses, were there to reinforce the religion's claim of truth. We may have been taught to revere a book like the Bible or Qur'an. We may have had requirements of diet, like fasting, or other rules about what we could not eat or simply have had the requirement to say our prayers at night. For most of us, the claims of truth were developed much more in religious practice than in any attempt at verifying it.

The practice that served most to convince us of faith in childhood was typically prayer. Particularly in theistic religions, we were taught to pray to a kind father figure. We were told that he cared for us, and in many cases, we spoke to him every night. A parent may have watched us as we said our nightly prayers. So our relationship with God was in many ways a parental relationship.

It is not that our parents were seeking to deceive us. They were simply passing on an unquestioned belief that had been passed on to them. They did so not just because they thought it was their duty but because they believed it was the loving thing to do. They wanted us to grow up to be happy and good people and were convinced that we needed religion to do that. However, good intentions do not make something true. But some of you reading this may think that no evidence is a 50/50 bet, and you might as well land on the side of belief. Consider this scenario:

> You are arrested for a murder you didn't commit. The victim was apparently gunned down from a passing vehicle, so there was no forensic evidence except the bullets, but as the weapon has not been found, that can't be traced back to anyone.

You can't prove where you were when the murder was committed. The murdered man lived near to you, but to the best of your knowledge, you never met him or had any association with him. But how can you prove that? How can you prove you have never met someone you live near to?

The police allege you slipped out of your house, got into an unidentified vehicle, put on leather gloves, used a gun with a silencer to kill the man, then passed the gun and gloves to the driver, who disposed of them. You then quietly slipped back into your home. That would all have been possible had you been the killer.

In the court, you can see from the faces of the jury that they believe you are guilty. Even your lawyer is sceptical. After all, you can't provide any evidence of your innocence. Now you could rely on faith, but you might as well hope that the jury will toss a coin and it will come down on your side.

However, the strongest point your sceptical lawyer has is that there is no evidence against you. There is no evidence you ever met the victim, no evidence you left your house at the time of the shooting, no evidence you ever got into that vehicle or held the gun used for the killing, and no evidence you are the killer.

Now which would you want the jury to go with, their belief or the absence of evidence? If you think belief is superior to the absence of evidence, you'd better hope there is no death sentence in our hypothetical legal jurisdiction. There is a good reason why courts in democratic countries look for evidence and not the absence of it. Where there is no evidence, we can do no more than guess. Having no evidence is not a sensible reason for believing that anything is true. However, there is still a form of special pleading that religions claims should give them a special diplomatic immunity from the normal rules of evidence. That is the claim of religious experience.

Chapter Eleven

THE RELIGIOUS EXPERIENCE

'Atheists just dismiss every experience they have never had as automatically untrue. They are closed to the wonders of spiritual experience.' How many times have we non-believers heard that assertion? How often have we been accused of simply ignoring the evidence? The argument is that we rely simply on intellectual arguments and that there is more to life than the intellectual. I have frequently encountered this objection to my arguments. My best response to this is to do something which is usually outside the scope of arguments against religion made by 'New Atheists', that is to explore one of my own spiritual experiences. I am not unique in this. Richard Carrier also addresses a spiritual experience (see http://www.infidels.org/library/modern/testimonials/carrier.html). I am going to explain why such experiences can be so convincing and why I eventually concluded that they are no more that products of the human mind.

I spent about a quarter of a century earnestly seeking 'spirituality'. I began this journey at the age of eighteen, after having already rejected my childhood religion a couple of years earlier, and continued it until I was in my early forties. I looked within Christianity and beyond it, particularly in Buddhism. I stayed in both Anglican and Buddhist monasteries. I read many of the writings of Krishnamurti (however far from all, as he was very prolific and repetitive). I passionately wanted to understand where spiritual truth lay. For years, I spent a period every morning reading the Bible, especially the psalms. Later, I spent a great deal of time meditating and keeping a spiritual journal. I was convinced I could find a profound spiritual truth.

As part of my spiritual journey, in my early twenties, I began to attend meetings of The Society of Friends, who are better known as Quakers. The Quakers are organised, but they have no formal religious leadership. They have no pastors and instead believe in the 'priesthood of all believers'. Their only form of worship is to meet together and sit in silence until someone present feels moved by the spirit to speak. Anyone attending is free to do so. I never formally became a

Quaker. However, it was at one of these meetings that I had a powerful 'spiritual' experience. I'm going to describe that as accurately as I can. I have put that as a quotation because it represents how I understood what happened then, rather than how I understand it now:

It was a bight spring Sunday morning, with early signs of blossom on the trees, when Marion (whom I was married to, for a period, in my twenties) and I walked the short distance to the Friends Meeting House, in Newcastle Upon Tyne. Inquiring into Quakerism had been more my idea than hers, but we were both exploring ideas that would lead to spiritual development.

Inside, we sat on wooden benches. They were placed in opposite rows. It struck me as more like the seating in the House of Commons than most churches. This was, after all, a meeting house. We sat through periods of silence, which were punctuated by someone briefly rising to speak. The silence seemed more powerful than the speaking. At first, I felt that I was being enveloped in it. It was a powerful force that was drawing me in.

But something changed; something grew out of that silence. The Holy Spirit came into me. It started as no more than a very slight tremble, then a light flutter in my stomach. I felt embarrassed and didn't want to speak, but I knew I would have to. Before I could give the matter much more thought, the flutter was growing into a powerful energy within me. It was filling my whole upper body. There was a tornado within me. I made no conscious decision to stand up, but it forced me to my feet.

To the best of my recollection, I quoted 1 Corinthians 13, 'If I speak in the tongues of men and of angels, but have not love, I am a noisy gong or a clanging cymbal.' And then said, 'For love is all that matters and is the only true measure of our life.' It was not I, but the spirit, who was choosing my words. I was just a vessel for the message.

But soon, too soon, I felt the spirit leaving me. I had nothing more to say and so sat down. As I did so, the spirit drained from me, then left me completely. That powerful, entrancing force had gone from my body. I felt deep joy at my experience, yet sorrow that it had passed so quickly.

The memory of the experience did not, however, leave me. It was the experience, of that force compelling me to rise and speak, that I found unforgettable. When I look back on it, I can see it had an intoxicating effect. For many years, I was to look on this as one of the most powerful experiences of my life. I wanted it again. I was convinced that the Holy Spirit, the God of the burning bush, the living spirit at the heart of all great religions, had briefly taken possession of me.

That was not the only powerful 'spiritual' experience I had, but it was that more than any other experience or belief which, for many years, convinced me that there was a truth at the heart of spirituality.

My experience is what is classed as a 'peak experience'. At its most celebrated, it is the experience of Paul, on the road to Damascus, or Moses, up the mountain. The term also describes the realisations of the Buddha and Muhammad. In more recent times, there was the peak experience of Bill Wilson, who went on to cofound Alcoholics Anonymous. However, most, like mine, are less dramatic and have little effect on the world. Those who have had them have produced much of the 'spiritual literature' of the world. They matter because they are at the heart of religion. They are often, in theist religions, seen as a way in which people are inspired by God.

Some of the most prominent attempts to analyse these experiences have been those Abraham H. Maslow in his book Religions, Values, and Peak-Experiences in 1964 and The Varieties of Religious Experience by William James in 1902.

James actively addresses the idea that the experiences often arise at a point of mental instability. That would apply in my case. It is, however, important to stress that 'spiritual experiences' are real experiences, just as having a dream is something that actually happens to us. The form they take may differ greatly. Mine was very different from someone 'speaking in tongues'. But I have no reason to believe it was any less intense. It should also be said that while there is a perception of a great spiritual force, I know of no verified case where anything that has happened is beyond normal physical possibilities. There is no verified evidence of anyone developing supernatural powers as a result of such experiences.

The convincing thing about these experiences is that they seem to be, I am sure, genuine experiences, which cannot be summoned at will. Indeed, if they were acts of the will, that would contradict their purpose. They are, however, pursued. That is hardly surprising since they have such a power over the mind.

I pursued them for more than twenty years, not just in Quakerism but elsewhere. I spent time in meditation in Buddhist monasteries, hoping meditation would bring me a similar breakthrough. I tried looking at that world from a Taoist approach. I'd watch videos of talks by Krishnamurti, trying to grasp where his charismatic power came from. Looking back on those, I now think what a bully he was. For years, I kept a spiritual journal, always seeking a great truth through self-awareness. I would have said I was looking for understanding but I was also seeking another spiritual high.

The least harmful of my experiences and those which can be most beneficial were meditation and self-awareness. These practices can be divorced from any belief system. They are a way of looking at our own thinking patterns rather than a doctrine or dogma. They may well help to enhance an already stable mind in some cases. However, the idea that they can lead to permanent mental stability in the case of serious mental illness is unproven. What seems more probable is they help some people to manage the condition. That can be a benefit, but in my case, it also fed into the condition and, at times, I became very obsessive. My most sane approach to the world unquestionably came gradually from abandoning all spiritual ideas and adopting an evidence-based approach to deciding what is true.

The link between mental illness and powerful spiritual experiences is widely accepted, and my most extreme experiences coincided with periods of deep mental instability. Peak experiences are extreme mental experiences. They are at the edge of awareness. I have felt that I had the joy of unity with all things (a great mental high), but these experiences arose from the mental discontinuity of a mind suffering from bipolar disorder. I have found it much easier to manage this condition free from any religious or spiritual ideas.

The theistic tradition has been to separate the human being into the physical, mental, and spiritual. The spiritual is seen as an innate aspect of humanity which needs awakening. This awakening is expressed by Martin Luther as quoted by William James in The Varieties of Religious Experience:

'When a fellow monk,' said Luther, 'one day repeated the words of the Creed: "I believe in the forgiveness of sins," I saw the scripture in an entirely new light; and straightforward I felt as if I were born anew. It was as if I had found the door of paradise thrown open.'

Peak experiences have been seen as a source of truth because the religious interpretation of them has been accepted. The problem is that interpretation is not a guide to what is true. I had realisation after realisation. There was a coherency within the rationale of those realisations, but that is not the same as an objective coherency. Luther sees scripture in an entirely new light. His understanding of it is transformed, but that is simply a psychological change within him. It is not a new discovery about the world.

The problem is that this type of realisation feels like it is a universal truth. It seems so deeply true when experienced that it appears to be obvious that once it is proclaimed, everyone else should see it as true. That type of certainty has contributed to a great deal of conflict, especially when linked to a situation of competing religious identities. That sense of certainty also often leads to conflict with others within a religion.

It is very clear from his letters that the apostle Paul (who is examined in more detail later) was a domineering man, who actively asserted his viewpoint after his conversion experience. Those letters which are identified as from Paul are filled with conflict.

There is no evidence that the appearance of personal transformation these experiences bring reflects any truly profound and lasting change. James quotes a passage from Luther, in his later years, which begins, 'I am utterly weary of life' (Varieties of Religious Experience). This suggests he had a depressive nature even after his pivotal role in the reformation.

The most convincing thing about many of these experiences is often their physicality. They are more than just thoughts. Howard Conder, the founder of Revelation TV, in a discussion with Richard Dawkins recounts a 'spiritual experience' and describes an incredible electrical force going into the small of his back and through his torso, like thousands of volts (about thirty minutes into interview) (http://www.youtube.com/watch?v=kk1RnwbFIps&feature=endscreen).

Conder's conviction, that he was filled with the power of the Holy Spirit, was so great that he went on to recount how a girl had been brought back to life, through that power. Richard Dawkins's polite response is remarkably restrained at that point. These are powerful physical experiences. The question anyone thinking that they come from the Holy Spirit, or any other force beyond the human mind, must answer is, how do you know?

The human body has many powerful yet unintentional reactions. When someone is very angry, heart rate and blood pressure can dramatically change. People in life-threatening situation can find a physical strength they would not normally possess. Dietary, sleep, and sensory deprivation appear to play a significant part in these experiences. Muhammad, Jesus, and Buddha, each went through a form of self-inflicted deprivation. Muhammad is said to have spent weeks alone in a dark cave. Jesus is said to have fasted in the dessert for forty days. The tradition is that the Buddha followed a number of severe ascetic practices, including near starvation. This brought him to the realisation of the middle way, which was to avoid the extremes. So why do the experiences that are seen as having the most effect on spiritual awakenings arise from such extreme physical and mental deprivation?

One argument might be that humans only reach a deep spiritual clarity at a point of physical and mental crisis. Jesus was tormented by the Devil, while fasting in the desert. The Buddha nearly starved himself to death. Muhammad sat alone for days in the darkness of a cave. Then each gets a realisation which is in accord with his cultural context. So the question is, do they reach that realisation by somehow reaching something beyond everyday human consciousness or is it that the mind throws them an image that allows them to end the deprivation?

In each case, what they find becomes the inspiration for a major religious tradition. But if what they had found was a profound universal truth, why would these religions differ so much? We have three accounts of men seeking the most profound understanding of human existence and yet three different answers—three answers which reflect the cultures they are in. The Buddha is then said to have rejected such extreme approaches and followed the 'middle way', but he still went through an extreme process to reach that point.

The pattern we can discern from these experiences is not that they were in any way fabricated but that there is a distinction between an experience being authentic and the content of that experience being true. Perception is not the same as truth. We need to ask a few simple questions about these experiences. If each of these men had set out to find profound spiritual truth, and it had an objective reality, we'd reasonably have expected them to all come up with similar results. As each came up with a development of what was already found within their culture, where is the evidence of divine intervention or profound awareness beyond normal human thought?

The gospels are written in the Roman world and reflect the emergence of a religion which comes out of Judaism. To a large extent, they depend on that religion. They repeatedly use the Old Testament as a source of authority. Buddhism emerges from Hinduism, and Islam arises from the Abrahamic tradition. In each case, the originality of the new religion is proclaimed as from a new form of spiritual knowledge, but there is nothing in any of them that is any more than the product of the mind's coping mechanisms. Each of these men came up with understanding that saved them from extreme mental and physical distress.

The peak experience, therefore, makes no sense as simply the source of profound awareness, but it does make sense as a survival strategy for a mind deeply imbued with religious ideas. It is hardly surprising that a mind tutored in religious understanding should conjure up a vision or understanding of a 'spiritual' nature at a point of crisis. It is the most powerful response the mind in crisis can throw up.

We have a fight or flight response which in some situations is overtaken by strong coping mechanism, which focuses the mind and allows people to act with a lot of clarity in a dangerous situation. We find that response to crisis in situations such as a fire or road accident. Peak experiences are responses to points of internal crisis within the mind. They occur in the mind of those close to some form of self-destruction.

One question is, why then did these figures have such an impact on the world? The answer to that, however, has more to do with the use of religion as a political tool than with any peak experience, a point which we will return to later. First, we'll look at one of the other factors that drives religion, that of religious identity.

Chapter Twelve

RELIGIOUS IDENTITY AND HATRED

One of the recurring themes of this book is religious identity. When we were children, many of us were told that we were Methodists, Muslims, Catholics, and so on. That identity usually defined our family. It may define our community and even our nationality. From early childhood, we are told that our religion defines who we are. Many of us had a ceremony in infancy to receive us into the religion. We may even have gone to schools that reinforced our faith.

The power of that identity depends on social and political circumstances, but religion can add an aspect that will often supersede any social or political factors and gives an enduring intensity to disputes that can make them effectively irresolvable, at least until religious feelings recede. When religion builds roadblocks, it constructs them with very powerful boulders. To understand how and why religion can be such a barrier to the resolution of disputes, we need to understand how religious identity develops.

We were taught religion in a very different way from how we are taught other subjects, such as geography or mathematics. We were taught it with an emotional context that goes to the core of our identity. We were taught that it is so important that it has a day set aside for it each week. We were taught we should say prayers at regular times, such as before we went to bed. Our rituals may have differed according to our faith, denomination, and family, but those of us introduced to religion as children were all essentially indoctrinated. A quick glance at the Oxford Dictionary gives us the definition for indoctrinate: teach (a person or group) to accept a set of beliefs uncritically.

That is how most of us were taught religion. Children are not taught that there might be a God. They are taught God is love and he made the world. As they get older, children are taught that evidence is necessary in Science and History; they are taught to think critically about a literary text, but religion is treated as being outside these requirements. It is seen as a matter of faith, and faith is not something that needs to be scrutinised. A faith only needs to be believed in to be valid. That leads to a very large distortion in human thought. It teaches people to put belief before evidence; that belief is more important than evidence. This can be very dangerous. It promotes a way of thinking that extends beyond the formally religious. Believers are not taught to examine the nature of their religious identity.

The best way to understand this identity is to consider how it develops, in its most stark form. We will take as our archetype a young boy born into a Presbyterian working-class family in Belfast who will be called Kyle and how that is mirrored in the upbringing of a Catholic boy who we will be called Sean.

From a very early age, Kyle knows that he is a Protestant and that there are other children who are Roman Catholics and that he is different from them. He, at first, does not understand what divides these religions, but from his early years, he knows there is a division. In fact, the existence of a division is one of his first religious understandings, and, as we will see, it is his most powerful one. Even at a very early age, his world is shaped by an awareness of that difference. He sees Roman Catholics as dangerous.

As Kyle grows older, he understands some of the differences between the religions. He understands that Presbyterians don't want the Pope telling them what to believe and that they don't pray to the Virgin Mary. If, as is often the case, he has little or no contact with Catholics, he will grow in suspicion of them and may even develop deep hostility towards them.

No more than a few hundred yards from Klye lives Sean, who was born to Catholic parents. Sean has the same limited understanding of the theological differences between their denominations as Kyle has. Both boys grow up in similar economic circumstances. While Klye supports Rangers, the traditionally Protestant Glasgow football club, Sean supports the traditionally Catholic team Celtic; both are fans of Manchester United in the English Premier league. Both are brought up with conservative religious attitudes that oppose abortion and gay marriage.

Kyle and Sean have very distinct political beliefs. Kyle is an Ulster Loyalist, and Sean is an Irish Republican. These might appear to be every bit as significant as their religious identities, and they are important, but it is religious identity that gives them their power. When people define who someone is in Northern Ireland, they do it by religion. While there has been a political settlement in Northern Ireland, the tension that remains on the streets is blatantly about religious identity.

In descriptions of tensions in Northern Ireland, the media have increasingly moved away from the terms Protestant and Catholic and have preferred terms like Unionist, Loyalist, Nationalist, and Republican, even in disputes over marches by the Orange Order. The Orange Order describes itself as a Protestant fraternity and states that 'civil and religious liberty is their primary objective'. Its purpose is to protect a religious identity.

The strongest objections to the marches often surround the manner in which they pass Catholic Churches, which is seen as deeply provocative. The anger against such marches comes from the feeling that such an overtly Protestant organisation has no place in an area where Catholics live. The Orangemen feel they should have the right to walk down any street in a place where they live. This is not an argument over noise abatement. It is a dispute between two religious identities that feel threatened.

It is a fiction to pretend that the hatred and anger that can arise, on both sides, is not about religious identity. It has been for hundreds of years, and changing the terminology does not alter that. This is not to say that every member of the Orange Order is filled with hatred for Catholics or that every Catholic hates in return.

Religious identity is at the heart of many conflicts around the world. The best way to understand it is expressed by the words, 'You can say what you want about me but don't ever insult my mother.' Except insulting a religious identity can be so much more intense. It is intense enough for people to be killed over the slightest of insults and passionate enough to last for generation after generation.

In religion, there is always a 'them and us'. This could also be said of politics, but what distinguishes religion is how that division is ingrained and regularly reinforced in childhood. Kyle and Sean go to different schools, and the difference between those schools is religion. That emphasises the difference of religion in the starkest way.

It is important to say that religious identity has no necessary relationship with religious devotion, but it is that which binds religion to intense conflicts. In many cases, but not all, those with a religious identity that leads them to violence don't have a long-standing strong religious devotion.

The two exceptions are in the case of the convert who needs devotion to confirm his new identity to himself or where devotion legitimises the act. There is evidence of Islamic terrorists becoming devout for a period of time before they act. With a few exceptions, there is no evidence that those involved in the Northern Irish conflict had a history of deep religious devotion.

This lack of devotion is why many argue that violence has nothing to do with religion. But the logic of their position is that religious identity has nothing to do with religion. They can't claim that and at the same time argue that community is a benefit of religion.

Religious identity is central to religion. It's an identity children are given at a very early age, and they are told it is their most important identity. It very often identifies their community. It often identifies the school they go to. More important, than any of this, it identifies the in-group and the out-group. This may not matter where there are no community tensions or conflicts that are seen as threatening a culture. However, where there is a division, it tells children who their enemy is. If you teach children they are a part of one group, who are different from another group, in the fundamental aspect of their identity and that they are threatened by that other group, don't be surprised if that sometimes leads to an intractable hatred. Religions often try to pretend that religious identity is in some way divorced from the religion itself, but it is religions that actively inculcate it. They actively reinforce the idea that a child is Catholic, Protestant, or Muslim and that that is their most important identity, and again and again fail to see how dangerous that can be.

RELIGIOUS HATRED

A group of men surround a mosque, chanting aggressively calling the worshippers 'dogs', 'thieves', 'terrorists', and 'black monsters'. This is part of a persecution of an Islamic community and a clear message that they are not welcome in the country. So who are the men who are shouting? In Britain, they could be supporters of one of the small Right Wing groups like the BNP (British National Party) or the ELD (English Defence League). In the USA, it could be an expression of hatred from a group of White Supremacists. It might be an outbreak of religious tensions in India. But it is none of the above. In this case, the hatred comes from Buddhists and comes from a movement led by Buddhist monks.

In Europe and North America, Buddhists are seen as the most benign of religions. Their leaders are men like the Dalai Lama who speaks softly, smiles broadly, and never utters any hatred, even against the Chinese invaders who drove him from his home. If you encounter a Buddhist monk or nun in any of the advanced industrial democracies, in cities like New York or London, they will probably be teaching a meditation class, giving a talk on Buddhism, or living quietly in a monastery. Lay Buddhists tend to be vegetarians, associated with ecological causes and generally living a peaceful life. They will be seeking to practise mindfulness and looking for harmony in their life. So the idea of an aggressive, violent Buddhism might seem like an oxymoron. Yet in Burma, the country of the celebrated winner of the Nobel Peace prize Aung San Suu Kyi, it is the case:

> Monks who played a vital role in Burma's recent struggle for democracy have been accused of fuelling ethnic tensions in the country by calling on people to shun a Muslim community that has suffered decades of abuse . . . have issued pamphlets telling people not to associate with the Rohingya community. (Independent.co.uk, 25 July 2012)

Religion exists in a social context. It divides humanity intensely because religious identity is fragile, and threatened identities are often a source of deep violence. Where a religion defines a nation's identity, those who do not adhere to it are often perceived as a threat to both the nation and the identity.

A common argument from believers is to cite wars which were not caused by religion and claim them as evidence that religion doesn't cause wars. It is a highly flawed form of argument. It is like identifying a cancer (such as prostate cancer) that is not caused by smoking and saying that it proves smoking does not cause cancer. The point is not that religion has caused every war in history. It does, however, play a significant part in many of the most persistent conflicts in the world and it unquestionably shapes their character. We can't begin to understand religious conflict without understanding religious identity and accepting how dangerous it is. I have set out a starting point for understanding the nature of religious identity. I offer a hypothesis that explains how it contributes to conflicts. They show how the most common aspects of religion lead into this pheromone.

CHARACTERISTICS OF RELIGIOUS IDENTITY IN CONFLICT SITUATIONS

Theses points sum up the significance of religious identity:

- Religion is, in most cases, a child's first identity and the identity considered as the most important by their parents.
- There is usually an initiation ceremony for the child. This, in some cases, is reinforced by later ceremonies such as bar mitzvah or confirmation usually around the years of early adolescence, seeking to ensure the child commits to that identity. In the case of Catholicism, the first communion has also served this function.
- Even in early childhood, children become aware that it is their religious identity that sets them aside from others. This is particularly true in a situation with a history of conflict. For example, a child of five in Northern Ireland knows she is Catholic and others are Protestants. A young child in India will know he is Hindu and others Muslim.
- It is an identity that is regularly reinforced, often with a day of the week set aside for that purpose. Religious schools and Sunday schools also foster identity.
- The acceptance of beliefs usually follows the religious identity rather the choice of religion following the beliefs. For example, people say, 'I believe this because I am a Christian, Muslim, etc.' instead of starting with a belief and seeking a religion in accord with it.
- Unlike a dispute over land or resources, which can be settled when one side wins or a compromise is agreed, as neither party in a religious conflict is willing to give up its beliefs, religious conflicts often have no solution.
- Religious identity is integral to religions as it is essential to the continuation of a religion. It is religious identity rather than the specific tenets of a religion that is passed from generation to generation. When a child marries out of a faith, the great rift that can occur between them and their parents is often because their parents feel that their grandchildren will not share their identity.

CONFLICTS WHERE RELIGIOUS IDENTITY IS NOT CENTRAL

The Second World War was the most total war in history; yet a mere five years after it ended, France, which had been invaded by Germany, made an extraordinary gesture of reconciliation. French Foreign Minister Robert Schuman proposed the Coal and Steel community, the starting point for the European Union. There was no continuation of violence between these nations. Despite the terrible nature of the war, they put it behind them.

While religion did clearly play a part in Hitler's hatred of the Jews, the conflict between France and Germany, which went back to the nineteenth-century conflict over the territory of Alsace-Lorraine, was not one over religious identity but over territory and political ideology.

There is a very simple, but profound, difference between a religious conflict, which often will include economic and territorial issues and disputes over purely political, economic, and territorial questions. You can resolve an economic or territorial dispute, as shown in the example above; after the Second World War, Alsace-Lorraine was returned to France and the matter was settled. Religious disputes are much more difficult to settle. In the case of a religious dispute even if the economic and territorial dispute is settled, it does not end the religious rancour. The creation of Pakistan did not end the enmity between Hindus and Muslims. Language disputes may not be wholly resolvable, but you can reach a manageable settlement. In places like Canada or Belgium, rules are created about the use of language, and even when linguistic identities are held with intensity, they are not usually a cause of intense violence, unless linked to religion.

The shooting at the Parti Québécois victory party in Montreal in September 2012 shows that language disputes can lead to violence. However, compared to the violence in religious disputes, these are very rare events, and there is no evidence of the level of bitter intercommunal strife you get in Northern Ireland or the Indian sub-continent.

Even the proposal for part of a country to secede can be handled without violence where the different between those parts of the state are not religious. At the time of writing, there is an agreement that a referendum over whether or not Scotland will leave the United Kingdom will be held. A vote to secede would be a major change for both Scotland and the rest of the United Kingdom, but it is not the cause of a violent dispute.

Yet consider the protracted and irresolvable disputes in the world, and religion again and again can be seen to play a significant role. The question we are faced with is what is it that makes disputes between religious identities the most enduring of disputes. We can find disputes over nationality, territory, language, and economics, which are resolvable, but are we seriously expected to believe that it is simply coincidence that the most difficult to resolve ones are of a religious nature? This chapter has established a correlation between religion and intractable conflicts, and it has gone further by showing that there is a strong case to show that the problem lies in the very nature of religion itself. The claim the 'Violent conflict has nothing to do with religion' simply does not stand up to scrutiny. Religion is the mother of religious identity, and religious identity is one of the most dangerous characteristics humans can have.

WHAT ABOUT THE EVIL ATHEISTS?

One of the arguments believers often make to justify the role of religion, in guiding human morality, is to proclaim that Atheism has killed millions of people. This is a deeply flawed argument for one simple reason. Belief is often a motivation for killing, not believing something isn't. We Atheists not only don't believe in the Christian God, but we also don't believe in Thor or Zeus. If we are to be associated with one God we don't believe in, why not all of them? Why only point out that we don't believe in the Abrahamic God?

If it makes sense to judge us for what we don't believe in, why does it not make equal sense to judge Christians or Muslims the same way? They don't believe in either Thor or Zeus. So if they use the confused logic that links us to Stalin or Pol Pot for not believing in the Abrahamic God, shouldn't they equally be linked to Stalin and Pol Pot because they share with Stalin and Pol Pot a non-belief in Thor and Zeus? Those who wish to use absurd logic should recognise how such absurdity can be equally applied to them.

One of the claims made is that Stalin and Pol Pot actively persecuted religions. They did. They did not, however, do so simply because of what they did not believe in. They persecuted religions because of what they did believe in. They both had political ideologies that did not tolerate opposition and saw religion, and many other factors in society, as opposing them. But they were following a long history of the suppression of religion. That, of course, is the history of one religion suppressing another. It should also be pointed out that Stalin, who had been taught in a seminary, had an ambivalent relationship with the Russian Orthodox Church. During the Second World War, there was active cooperation between the church and Soviet state (see http://www.russian-crafts.com/customs/russian-church-history.html).

However, there was, unquestionably, repression of the Russian Orthodox Church at other times. So we do have examples of regimes that oppress religion because of a political ideology and those that have done so for religious reasons. I have yet to find any example of a regime that suppressed religion because of what it did not believe in.

BUT WHAT ABOUT HITLER?

There is an argument over Hitler's Catholicism. What we do know is he was baptised and raised a Catholic, though how devout he was is disputed; that the church, as stated earlier, never excommunicated him; that he made statement after statement in Mein Kampf claiming that defending Christianity was one of his primary political goals; that the belts on soldiers, in Hitler's Germany, had the words Gott Mituns, 'God with us', on the buckle. None of this is a matter of dispute.

In opposition to this, it has been claimed that he made anti-Christian statements in private discussions with other Nazis. The source of these claims is immediately problematic. These documents collected in Table Talk did not emerge until after the war, and the source for them, Martin Borman (who'd been Hitler's private secretary) and the other transcribers Heinrich Heim and Henry Picker, had every reason to doctor them. Just as unfortunate for their credibility, they were authenticated by the Oxford University Historian Hugh Trevor-Roper, who later authenticated a set of diaries claimed to be 'Hitler's diaries' that were shown, by forensic examination, to be entirely forged. As Richard Carrier points out:

> Nowhere does Hitler denounce Jesus or his own brand of Christianity.

And

> The 'anti-Christian' portions of Table-Talk does not concur with Hitler's actions for 'positive' Christianity. (http://www.nobeliefs.com/ HitlerSources.htm)

So there is a question mark over the accuracy of Table Talk. However, even in the unlikely event that these were true accounts, it remains the case that Hitler never made any public statement saying he was leaving the Catholic Church. Much more important than Hitler's attitude towards the Catholic Church is the attitude the church had towards him.

The first treaty the government of Adolf Hitler signed was the Concordat (Reichskonkordat), a treaty between the Holy See and the German state. The signatories where Franz Von Papen, the vice-chancellor, and Cardinal Eugenio Pacelli, who was, at that time, the Vatican's secretary of state.

As anyone who has studied Adolf Hitler's rise will know, Von Papen was as former Chancellor of the Weimar Republic one of the politicians who joined in coalition with Hitler, thereby allowing the Nazis to come to power. It seems probable that the reason he, and not Hitler signed this treaty, may have been because it would have made it easier for Hitler to disavow it, had he wished to.

Cardinal Pacelli was an experienced Papal diplomat. He entered into this agreement, on behalf of his church, because he saw it as the best way to protect its interests. There is no justification that he did so out of naivety about German politics. He had been the Apostolic Nuncio to Germany throughout the 1920s and watched every twist and turn of the Weimar Republic. He had watched the rise of the Nazis and understood that their platform was deeply anti-Semitic.

The essence of the agreement was that the church would stay out of German politics and the German state would leave the church alone. Pacelli had worked closely with Fr Ludwig Kaas, the priest who had led Zentrum, the Catholic Centrist party. There had been opposition to Hitler from liberal Catholics and some bishops. These bishops had, in a number of cases, banned Catholics from joining the Nazi Party. Kaas had taken a pragmatic view and unlike the Social Democrats, decided, in March 1933, to support the Enabling Act, which effectively gave Hitler dictatorial powers. After doing so, he visited Pacelli in Rome to explain the situation. It is important to state that there is no evidence of Pacelli opposing that decision. The Catholic Church actively consented to Hitler becoming a dictator.

Within days, the bans that bishops had imposed on membership of the Nazi Party were lifted. So the Catholic Church now told the faithful it was OK to be a Nazi. This idea was compounded by the Concordat requiring newly consecrated bishops to swear an oath of allegiance to the German state, and the shared distrust of the Jews found in both Nazism and Christian teaching.

In the Summer of 1938, the Catholic Church, under the auspices of the now dying Pope Pius XI, in a weak attempt to counter the Nazi case for anti-Semitism, produced an encyclical calling for the unity of humanity. To what extent Pacelli was the author is unclear. Humani Generis Unitas (The Unity of the Human Race) was in fact dripping with anti-Semitism.

> Moreover, by a mysterious Providence of God, this unhappy people, destroyers of their own nation, whose misguided leaders had called down upon their own heads a Divine malediction, doomed, as it were, to perpetually wander over the face of the earth, were nonetheless never allowed to perish, but have been preserved through the ages into our own time. No natural reason appears to be forthcoming to explain this age-long persistence, this indestructible coherence of the Jewish people. (http://www.bc.edu/dam/files/research_sites/cjl/texts/cjrelations/resources/education/humani_generis_unitas.htm)

Frankly, these nasty, vicious sentiments could have as easily come from Mein Kampf. The most powerful indication of the collective church's approval of the Concordat came the following year, 1939, when Cardinal Pacelli was made Pope taking the title Pius XII. The Pope, himself, was saying it was OK to be a Nazi, and many Catholics became very active Nazis. The effect is found in the darkest chapter of the history of the Second World War:

> At least 500 former soldiers were incorporated into the SS in Auschwitz. The main religious affiliations stated by the guards were: Catholic (42.6%), Protestant (36.5%), and gottgläubig ('believer in God') (20.1%). (http://www.massviolence.org/Auschwitz?artpage=5)

After the Second World War, the Catholic Church repudiated Nazism. That was too late, far too late. Had they returned to position of those bishops who had opposed the Nazis, at an earlier date, the harm may have been less. But it is the figure of Catholic SS guards that shows the real harm. They were the ones who actively carried out the Holocaust. No SS guard was ever excommunicated for being one. The

Catholic Church may argue that it did not approve of all their actions, but it is beyond question that it actively consented to their participation in the Nazi Project.

It is argued that the now Pius XII personally helped many Jews. That may have saved his conscience, but it did not undo the tremendous damage of telling Catholics it was acceptable to be a Nazi.

The moral position of the Catholic Church was that it was the church of Christ and that to protect the interests of the church was to protect Christ's message to the world. But that is not where the responsibility of the Roman Catholic Church and wider Christianity ends.

One of the most striking things about the quote from Humani Generis Unitas above is that the Catholic Church was so steeped in anti-Semitism that they could not even recognise it when they put it in a document which was calling for humanity to be valued. The Catholic Church must take responsibility for this attitude. Virulent anti-Semitism was certainly not confined to Catholicism, alone. This hatred, also, had a strong history in Protestantism. Their anti-Semitism is traceable to attitudes that go back to the Reformation.

> Therefore be on your guard against the Jews, knowing that wherever they have their synagogues, nothing is found but a den of devils in which sheer self-glory, conceit, lies, blasphemy, and defaming of God and men are practiced most maliciously and veheming his eyes on them. (Martin Luther, On the Jews and Their Lies)

It is easy to say the Holocaust happened because Hitler was evil. He certainly was. However, if you ask why so many people cooperated with the Final Solution, you cannot ignore Christianity's long history of anti-Semitism. Contempt and hatred for the Jews had been endemic in Europe for many centuries. That was actively fostered by both Protestant and Catholic Christianity, with its religious myths. At the heart of that hatred was the grotesque myth that all Jews were tainted with the responsibility for the death of Christ. It was not Hitler who first saw simply being Jewish as a crime. Christianity had invented and fostered that ugly prejudice over many centuries. When bad times had fallen on countries across Europe, there'd been the cry it was being punished for tolerating the killers of Christ. Jews had been murdered and driven from their home with impunity.

Hitler used those myths to incite hatred, but he could not have done so had they not already been a product of religious belief. He dug into a deeper and more fertile soil of prejudice than is often recognised. The terrible truth is that even some of those who opposed his measures shared some of his prejudice. Perhaps the most famous and evocative words of opposition within the German state came from Pastor Martin Niemöller. They go something like:

First they came for the Socialists, and I did not speak out—
Because I was not a Socialist.
Then they came for the Trade Unionists, and I did not speak out—
Because I was not a Trade Unionist.
Then they came for the Jews, and I did not speak out—
Because I was not a Jew.
Then they came for me—and there was no one left to speak for me.

The problem is these were spoken words and accounts of them vary. In some versions, 'Then they came for the Jews' is 'Then they came for the Jehovah Witnesses.'

Harold Marcuse of UC Santa Barbara investigated the question.

In 1976 Niemöller was asked about the quotation in an interview. The Martin Niemoeller Foundation in Germany takes his 1976 answer to be definitive [see: http://www.martin-niemoeller-stiftung.de/4/daszitat]. In his lengthy answer Niemoeller mentioned the following groups, and claimed that he started using the quotation only recently (namely at a 1974 event, which is demonstrably untrue, since it appeared in print as early as 1955, based on a 1951 interview with someone who quoted it):

Communists
Trade Unions
Social Democrats

Jews who had become Protestant ministers (Niemoeller speaks of 'Judenstämmlinge'—Jews by lineage). (http://www.history.ucsb.edu/ faculty/marcuse/niem.htm)

So the original quote did not apply to all Jews. It refers to those with a Jewish origin who had become Christian. This version doesn't include Catholics or the press. In those cases, it could be argued this was a shortened form, but specifically choosing to only mention Jews who were confessing Christians is not an omission, it is a selection.

Saul Friedländer says:

But the steadfastness of the confessing church regarding the Jewish issue was limited to support of the rights of non-Aryan Christians. And even on this point Martin Niemöller was abundantly clear, for example in his 'Propostions on the Aryan Question' (Saetze zur Arierfrage) published in November 1933 that only theological consideration prompted him to take this position. As he was to state in his 1937 trial for criticism of the regime, defending converted Jews 'was uncongenial to him'.

Martin Niemöller goes on to talk about how the duty to the community of all Christians:

> . . . requires of us, who as a people had to carry a heavy burden as a result of the influence of the Jewish people . . . (Saul Friedlander, Nazi Germany and the Jews: The Years of Persecution, 1933-1939, Vol. 1)

Friedlander also quotes from Dietrich Bonhoeffer, the other prominent anti-Nazi pastor, who declared of the April 1933 Boycott of Jewish businesses:

> In the Church of Christ we have never lost sight of the idea that the 'Chosen People', who nailed the Saviour of the world to the cross, must bear the curse of the action through a long history of suffering.

We, therefore, can't begin to understand the Holocaust unless we acknowledge the deep anti-Semitism that lay at the heart of both Catholic and Protestant Christianity. The churches have since moderated their positions. In the case of the Catholic Church which has now officially rejected anti-Semitism, it would seem not unreasonable that they felt a degree of shame over their Nazi deal, if you thought that you'd be wrong. In 2009, Pope Benedict XVI declared Pius XII as venerable, thereby putting him on the path to sainthood.

Chapter Thirteen

WHY AN ALL POWERFUL, ALL LOVING, ALL-KNOWING GOD MAKES NO SENSE, NO MATTER WHAT WAY YOU ARGUE FOR ONE

If you are beginning to think that the more we look at religion the less sense it makes, let's consider further how religions construct their view of the world. Prof. John C. Lennox in debate with Richard Dawkins argued that faith in Jesus is based on historical evidence and is not essentially different from any other historical fact (see http://www.youtube.com/watch?v=GKP3tMlg0II).

Let's start by examining the idea that the existence of God is a fact. The story Abrahamic religions (Christianity, Islam, and Judaism) tell about the creation of the world is simple: an all-powerful (omnipotent), all-knowing (omniscient), and all-loving (omnibenevolent) God made it. While it is true that those within these religions differed on the how literal the creation myth is and the role of the Big Bang, or evolution, in the story, they all start from the idea that it began with a God with these qualities. They claim that God is ultimately responsible for the universe.

They further agree that love comes from God, and God is the definition of love. The evil in the world, or at least in humanity, comes from human wickedness and the rejection of God. They will argue this rejection of God is the result of decisions that humans have taken using their own 'free will', and therefore, humanity is responsible for its own misfortune. Again, the way they construct this argument differs. However, the essence is that God is pure goodness which humanity has strayed away from.

This is a story that makes absolute claims, and it, therefore, needs to be shown to be true in all elements without self-contradiction. If a claim is eternally true, it needs to be so in every part and at all times. That is not a standard I am setting but reflects the nature of the claim believers make. As we will see, all elements of the claim cannot be true, and every time believers try to defend one or two of the elements of it they have to sacrifice some other claims about God. They can never show all aspects of these claims about God to be simultaneously true. We are now going to look at why these are a set of claims that make no sense no matter how they are argued.

Let's start with the first claim that God is all powerful (omnipotent). An all-powerful God could do anything. Now, the odd thing is that believers at this point often jump up with an objection. I mention this here because it is a very common objection raised by believers and needs to be directly dealt with. They say yes God is all powerful, but after he created the laws of physics, he decided not to change them, and he chose not to in order to allow the world to be consistent. He has only occasionally interfered to perform miracles that demonstrate his magnificence. Believers love to take the argument down this track, but this argument is not valid. It is irrelevant.

Let me be clear, what happened after God supposedly created the laws of physics is irrelevant. What matters is the nature of the decision to create them, in the first place. If God did not create the laws of physics and did not have the power to create them differently from the way they were created, the laws of physics would not be subject to God. He would be subject to them. God would, therefore, not be all powerful. Physics would be all powerful. The case for God, as described above, would immediately collapse.

So we have established that for this story to be true, God would have had to have been entirely free in how he created existence. That means he could use any mechanism he wanted and create the world, and all that is in it, any way he wanted. That would have to apply to everything in existence. Otherwise, he would not be an all-powerful God. So, arguments about God self-imposing limitations, after he made the world, are not relevant to this question.

It is important to be clear about the term 'all knowing'. An all-knowing God would know everything that has ever happened and everything that will ever happen. He would know your every private thought and keep a record of it, presumably in his phenomenal memory. It would, after all, be a necessity in most (though not all) versions of the entrance examination for Heaven.

Now when you think about the kind of record God would need to keep, it does not sound very loving. It frankly just sounds plain, creepy, and intrusive. It suggests the ultimate stalker rather than the ultimate kind and loving parent. It is important to also note that knowledge like that means it can't be claimed that God ever has the excuse that he didn't know the consequences of his decisions. All knowledge, after all, must mean a full knowledge of the future and of every consequence of every decision.

That knowledge would have to mean that before deciding to make the world, God would have known of every abused child, including those who would plead with him for help. He'd have known of everyone who would starve to death. He'd know everyone who would die violently. God had the choice to create a world where these things would happen. If he is all powerful, he could have created a world without such terrible suffering. He would have to have had that choice because that is what being all powerful means.

Believers reading this may, at this very moment, be leaping to their feet and shouting that 'God is innocent. Free will is to blame for the cruelty in the world.' That is a very weak objection because if God created the world, it would have been his choice to allow 'free will' or not. If he did not have that choice, he'd not be all powerful.

Ah, but there is the objection that free will is a necessity. If it was necessary, God would not be all powerful. He would be governed by the need for free will. I visualise the believer with admirable persistence conjuring up a further objection. Love is only possible if there is free will. That is another attempt to argue that God could not have done things differently. This argument fails again because God would not be all powerful if he could not create a world with love, without cruelty. I should point out that this is an argument over a supposed God's decision to create 'free will', and not over whether or not free will exists. That argument is in the province of those who care for philosophical abstractions that make the vagaries of the fate of Schrodinger's cat seem pedestrian. That is not a question this book will get lost in.

Let's make this simple. Either God freely chose how he'd create the world, and knew the outcome, or he didn't. If a believer argues he was in any way hampered in his freedom, they are arguing he is not omnipotent. To argue that God, in any way, did not know what the outcome would be is to argue that he is not omniscient.

Those who seek to enter the plea that God is not responsible for the outcome of 'free will' need to explain why God knowingly decided to allow free will when he knew the suffering that the exercise of it would cause to the victims of it. Why did he consider it more important to give free will to the murderer, child abuser, or thief than create a world where their victims would be protected? If there is sin in a world created by this all-powerful God, it was his choice to allow it. It could not have been there without his will. If all powerful, he could have created the world otherwise. How was it loving of God to knowingly and intentionally create a world with sin in it?

So we come to the third claim that God is all loving and therefore all good (omnibenevolent). What do we mean by loving? We mean caring for the welfare of others. When we love someone, we want them to be happy and healthy, and we behave in a caring way towards them. For instance, we would not knowingly create a situation where someone we loved would suffer and suffer seriously. That would not be love. Yet that is the outcome of our simple story of how God created the world.

If we knowingly act in a way that causes harm, we are responsible. Yet none of us can fully know what the results of our actions will be. The drunk driver is held responsible for getting behind the wheel of a car, yet, at that point, he or she does not know who the car will injure or kill or if anyone will be hurt. But knowledge of the consequences of your actions gives you a responsibility for them. The God which theists believe in created a world knowing exactly what the outcome would be. To precisely know that an action is going to lead to terrible harm, before you do it, is not supreme love, it is supreme culpability and callousness. The theist God is not a God of love but a God of cruel irresponsibility. He intentionally created a world knowing all the suffering that would be in it.

THE ROYAL FLUSH

There is, of course, one last answer that believers give to all this, and they tend to present it with the confidence of a poker player who is certain they have an unbeatable royal flush. They may not actually say 'Read 'em and weep,' but that is how confident they are of their answer.

Their argument goes that God did knowingly and intentionally create a world in which he would not directly cause suffering but allowed it to happen. He did this because he had to allow a world of good and evil for a higher purpose. They say that no one can know or comprehend the mind of God and that everything he does comes from a love beyond human understanding. So God's motives were good, and we have no right to question them. There are believers who like to use a line of argument that denies there is any right to question the claims made about God. OK, let's see if this hand is a royal flush or a busted flush.

Let's examine the claim that God has a higher purpose that we mere humans can't understand, with reference to Christianity. We are told, by Christians, that human love should be a reflection of God's love for us. The nature of God's love is explained in the gospels. We are given examples of how we should love our neighbour as our self. One of the most well-known illustrations, of this, is the story of the Good Samaritan. Let's see what that story tells us.

> And Jesus answering said, A certain man went down from Jerusalem to Jericho, and fell among thieves, which stripped him of his raiment, and wounded him, and departed, leaving him half dead. And by chance there came down a certain priest that way: and when he saw him, he passed by on the other side. And likewise a Levite, when he was at the place, came and looked on him, and passed by on the other side. But a certain Samaritan, as he journeyed, came where he was: and when he saw him, he had compassion on him, And went to him, and bound up his wounds, pouring in oil and wine, and set him on his own beast, and brought him to an inn, and took care of him. And on the morrow when he departed, he took out two pence, and gave them to the host, and said unto him, Take care of him; and whatsoever thou spendest more, when I come again, I will repay thee. Which now of these three, thinkest thou, was neighbour unto him that fell among the thieves? And he said, He that shewed mercy on him. Then said Jesus unto him, Go, and do thou likewise. (Luke 10: 30-37)

Now this is a heart-warming story of human kindness. However, the Samaritan is not recorded as saying to the man that his suffering is for a higher purpose. Surely that would have reflected God's love as explained in the 'royal flush'. What the Good Samaritan did was to show concern for the robbed man, give him practical help, and ensure he was cared for. That is how the gospel tells us God defines love.

So how was it loving for God to knowingly and intentionally create a world where the man would be beaten and robbed in the first place? Either God's definition of love is as explained in this parable or it isn't. It does not make sense to argue that creating the conditions and knowingly giving the robbers the free will to attack and rob the man was a loving decision. They are the opposite to the actions of the Samaritan. Christians love to talk about God as a loving father, but what loving father would create a situation where he knew, and knew with absolute certainty, that his children would be harmed, when he had the power to prevent it?

The simple reality is that there is no way to fit the triangle of the God of love, knowledge, and power together. They don't fit. There simply is no coherent explanation for a God who is all powerful, all loving, and all knowing. Now let's address the question whether the Bible makes sense.

WHY BIBLE THEOLOGY
IS BIBLE MYTHOLOGY

Chapter Fourteen

Two Gods, Four Authors, and an Editor

One way in which many people find freedom from religion is to start by understanding that they have been sold something which is very different from that advertised. One of the big claims about the Abrahamic God is that he is not the product of a mythical story like the Greek God Zeus or the Nordic God Thor. Another is that there has always been the belief that there is only one God. This is a central claim of the three Abrahamic religions of Christianity, Islam, and Judaism. All three of them claim descent from a single God. In Islam, the statement 'There is no God but Allah' (the word Allah is simply Arabic for God) is the central tenet of the faith. No question is asked about the origins of that God. He is simply assumed to have always existed.

All three faiths believe this single God created the world and see the central figure of Abraham as a patriarch (hence the term Abrahamic). In Judaism, he is the founding father of the faith; in Islam, his name is Ibrahim and he is the first Muslim. In Christianity, he is an important early Prophet who is venerated as an example of unswerving faith (an idea we will be dissecting later).

The God of Abraham is seen as the God of Adam before him and the God of Jacob after him. Nothing could be more simple or central to all three faiths than the claim that there was always only one God and there would always be one. However, it isn't that simple, and the origin of God lies in myths.

The most accurate way to describe religion in early Judaism was henotheistic, which means they worshipped one God but did not deny the existence of other ones. Their position could be best summed up as their God was better than other gods. Moses expresses this point in Exodus 15: 11.

> Who among the gods
> is like you, Lord?
> Who is like you—
> majestic in holiness,
> awesome in glory,
> working wonders?

The biblical scholar and professor of Jewish studies Richard Elliot Friedman said:

> It is a strange fact that we have never known with certainty who
> produced the book that played such a central role in our civilization. (Who
> Wrote the Bible? (1988))

He explains why many of the traditional claims for who wrote it make no sense. For instance, Moses is seen as the author of the Pentateuch (the first five books of the Bible). There are a number of reasons why this makes no sense. We find one glaring absurdity in Deuteronomy, the last of these books. It gives us an account of the Moses's death. It even tells us what happened after he died.

> And the children of Israel wept for Moses in the plains of Moab
> thirty days: so the days of weeping and mourning for Moses were ended.
> (Deut. 34: 8)

Leaving aside the apparently after-death compositions (or should that be decompositions) of Moses, Friedman provides a very coherent case for four different authors and an editor of these five books. He demonstrates this by showing how these authors tell different and contradictory stories within the text, which shows they differ in their understanding of God's character and how he relates to, and communicates with, humanity.

Friedman refers to the nineteenth scholar Karl Heinrich Graf who, working on the biblical texts and earlier research, identified four authors:

- The author who used the divine name Yahweh or Jehovah he called J.
- The author who used the term God (in Hebrew, Elohim) he called E.
- The author with Priestly references (almost certainly a priest) he called P.
- The author of the Book of Deuteronomy he called D.
- Finally, there was an editor who wielded the versions together.

This explains why so many parts of the early Bible are repeated and the versions contradict each other. It is why we have two versions of the creation story, the flood, and even of the Ten Commandments. It is a very direct challenge to the claim that the Bible is the infallible and unerring word of God, as many evangelical Christians claim. It is not just an amalgamation of different versions of a traditional story. In its earliest parts, it is an amalgamation of two different gods.

The kingdoms of Judah and the region that was to become Israel had different Gods. Yahweh was the God of Judah; El was the God of Israel. Both were male patriarchal gods. However, they even differed in how they were patriarchal. El could be compared to the Greek God Zeus, for he sat as the head of a council of gods. Yahweh was not described in terms of myths but through his historical acts.

It is worth stopping and considering what is being claimed here. We are overturning the central plank of the three monotheistic religions. We must, therefore, be very clear about why the idea of one God is being challenged. This is not a claim that should be made lightly or on flimsy evidence. It is important to say that the idea is being challenged not by an opposing belief system but on the basis of the evidence provided by the Bible itself.

Karen Armstrong (A History of God, 1993) traces the history of El from Babylonian beliefs to the Canaanite High God of the fourteenth century BCE who was married to Asherah and heads up a council which is divided by a conflict between the gods. Yes, God having a wife doesn't fit with what you may have heard in church, synagogue, or mosque. Let's keep going. The next bit might need rereading, but it is important.

The Bible uses five different terms for God: Yahweh, Jehovah, Elohim (El), God, and significantly the phrase 'LORD God' (with the word Lord always in upper case letters).

Yahweh and Jehovah are held to be variations of the same name, with Jehovah simply being a translation. They are distinct, in this part of the Bible, from the terms El or God.

The term 'LORD God' (Jehovah) is unmistakeably an identification of the great authority figure in the Bible. We are going to look at how it is distinct, in the early Bible, from the term 'God' (El).

The first thing we need to look at is how the Book of Geneses weaves together two separate and distinct accounts of the creation story. We can see how crudely they have been sewn together. We can identify the competing accounts of the J and E authors and see that separately they make coherent stories. Whereas stitched together, they are the contradictory mess that makes up the earliest part of the Bible. We'll start by looking at Genesis stories of how God and LORD God each created man and woman.

We find the God version in Genesis 1: 25-27 from the KJV:

> And God made the beast of the earth after his kind, and cattle after
> their kind, and every thing that creepeth upon the earth after his kind: and
> God saw that it was good. And God said, Let us make man in our image,
> after our likeness: and let them have dominion over the fish of the sea, and
> over the fowl of the air, and over the cattle, and over all the earth, and over
> every creeping thing that creepeth upon the earth. So God created man

in his own image, in the image of God created he him; male and female created he them.

We find the LORD God version in Genesis 2: 7-8, 18-23 from the KJV:

And the Lord God formed man of the dust of the ground, and breathed into his nostrils the breath of life; and man became a living soul. And the Lord God planted a garden eastward in Eden; and there he put the man whom he had formed.

*   *   *

And the LORD God said, It is not good that the man should be alone; I will make him an help meet for him. And out of the ground the LORD God formed every beast of the field, and every fowl of the air; and brought them unto Adam to see what he would call them: and whatsoever Adam called every living creature, that was the name thereof. And Adam gave names to all cattle, and to the fowl of the air, and to every beast of the field; but for Adam there was not found an help meet for him. And the Lord God caused a deep sleep to fall upon Adam, and he slept: and he took one of his ribs, and closed up the flesh instead thereof; And the rib, which the Lord God had taken from man, made he a woman, and brought her unto the man. And Adam said, This is now bone of my bones, and flesh of my flesh: she shall be called Woman, because she was taken out of Man.

So in the first version, 'God' first made the beasts of the Earth, the cattle, and the insects (yes, humanity came after insects), and then after he saw that was good, he decided to make man, by which we can infer he meant humanity, as a whole, because he made man and woman together.

In the second version, 'LORD God' starts by making man (a single male) out of the dust of the ground, which was hardly from his own image. How often do you get a preacher comparing man made from dust and man made in God's image in the same sermon?

Eventually, he thinks the poor fellow is lonely, so he creates some cattle and birds to keep him company. Then Adam wanders round naming all the creatures (well, what else could he do?). Oddly, that just doesn't meet his needs. So LORD God, ever wanting to be helpful, administers an unspecified anaesthetic to him and then, while he is unconscious, performs a costectomy (the removal of a rib) and transforms the excised body part into a woman.

These are very different stories and they tell of different gods. In the first, God creates all the conditions for humanity to survive in and then creates both the male and female parts of humanity. In the second, there is a clear message of male supremacy not just over women but over the whole planet. While in the first, the beasts and animals are already there before the people; in the second, Adam is created, then the animals and Eve are specifically created for him. The LORD God seems far from all knowing. He needs to experiment with the world. He is not knowledgeable of human needs, well, certainly not about sexual needs.

Christian apologists have come up with various weak excuses for these contradictions. One of the main lines of argument goes back to James Orr, the nineteenth-century Scottish theologian, in God's Image in Man and Its Defacement in the Light of Modern Denials (1905). This argument is worth considering because it illustrates how tenuous some of the arguments for religion can be.

Orr argued that the different versions were one narrative which is bound together by a commentary. The first account is an overall introduction, and the second gives us detail. He argues that this was a common approach. He explains away the different names for God, in an earlier work:

> . . . the truth, namely, that God is plurality as well as unity—that in
> Him there is a manifoldness of life, a fullness and diversity of powers and
> manifestation, such is as expressed in the word Elohim. (The Christian
> View of God and the World, James Orr (1893))

Elohim for him is not the name of an alternative God but an expression of the nature of God. The problem with this is it simply doesn't answer the flat contradictions in the text. His justification for this claim is that you find this style of giving an account of history on a royal inscription in Urartu, in the mountainous plateau between Asia Minor and Mesopotamia. That really is clutching at a straw.

You have to ask what a royal inscription in Asia Minor has to do with how the ancient Hebrews recorded their history. For this to be the equivalent of the account we find in Genesis, it would need to first state a general had lost a battle and then give an account of him winning it in the detail. It is like someone in a few hundred years coming across a twentieth-century English graveyard and concluding that 'beloved' was the commonest form of endearment in twentieth-century speech and that the dates of someone's birth and death were considered the most important things about them, and then assuming the same term 'beloved' was used in France.

This reflects the great lengths Christian apologists will go to fit the square peg of the Bible into the round hole of history. Because they are certain their belief is correct, they often grasp at any straw of historical information and seek to use it to put an imagined roof on the structure they claim their belief provides. Deep conviction can be a great barrier to objectively assessing historical claims. And time has not made their case any better. Josh McDowell in The New Evidence That Demands a Verdict (1999) quotes the example of the royal inscription from Urartu as part of his evidence that Moses was the author of the all five books of the Pentateuch. Well, if you have got a good story, you have to keep telling it, and never mind how valid it is.

Chapter Fifteen

GOD'S WIFE

It is hard to judge any marriage from the outside, but we can only conclude that God's marriage wasn't happy, if we look at how he later tried to deny he ever had a wife. There were plenty of leading religious figures who were keen to help. Not least of these was the prophet Jeremiah.

> 15 Then all the men who knew that their wives had made offerings to other gods, and all the women who stood by, a great assembly, all the people who lived in Pathros in the land of Egypt, answered Jeremiah: 16 'As for the word that you have spoken to us in the name of the Lord, we will not listen to you. 17 But we will do everything that we have vowed, make offerings to the queen of heaven and pour out drink offerings to her, as we did, both we and our fathers, our kings and our officials, in the cities of Judah and in the streets of Jerusalem. For then we had plenty of food, and prospered, and saw no disaster. 18 But since we left off making offerings to the queen of heaven and pouring out drink offerings to her, we have lacked everything and have been consumed by the sword and by famine.' 19 And the women said,[b] 'When we made offerings to the queen of heaven and poured out drink offerings to her, was it without our husbands' approval that we made cakes for her bearing her image and poured out drink offerings to her?' (Jer. 44: 15-19)

When confronted by Jeremiah for what he sees as idolatrous worship of 'the queen of Heaven', the women defend their actions by saying they are following what was done by 'our fathers, our kings, and our officials, in the cities of Judah and in the streets of Jerusalem'. They are stating they are returning to an established Jewish practice. They are blaming their misfortune on having neglected it. The object of their worship is the queen of Heaven. A queen is either the mother, wife of a monarch, or a monarch in her own right. We can exclude the possibility of this referring to Mary, the mother of Jesus, as it might do in much later Christian times. We can exclude the idea of a heavenly female monarch, entirely in her own right, as we have no evidence of that. We are left with the only possibility being that God had a wife, who was worshipped by some Jews. Further evidence tells the name of this Goddess was Asherah.

> The worship of Asherah in the northern kingdom of Israel endured until 721 BC, and even then in one corner of it, Beth-el, for we hear how Josiah, King of Judah (636-609 BC), destroyed the altars that had been set up by Jeroboam 300 years before and how he 'burned Asherah' (2 Kings 23: 15). (The Myth of the Goddess: Evolution of an Image, Anne Baring and Jules Cashford, Penguin Books, 1991.)

The reference to 'burning Asherah' is to burning the poles erected as part of the worship of the goddess.

Bible scholar Dr Francesca Stavrakopoulou made an excellent documentary on this (see https://www.youtube.com/watch?v=VtEsQT5M2IQ).

> Archaeological and genetic data support that both Jews and Palestinians came from the ancient Canaanites, who extensively mixed with Egyptians, Mesopotamian and Anatolian peoples in ancient times. Thus, Palestinian-Jewish rivalry is based in cultural and religious, but not in genetic, differences. (http://www.stml.net/text/Populations.pdf)

Asherah was a Canaanite/Babylonian Goddess. One reason for her rejection was clearly the establishment of patriarchal monotheism; the new single male God had no need of a wife. He was to be an unadulterated symbol of male power. Asherah may also have been a victim of the desire to establish a separate Hebrew identity. The genetic closeness of the Hebrews and the other Canaanites, they separated themselves from, suggests that the fierceness of the conflicts may be in part explained by the intensity often found in civil wars. Asherah was hated because she was seen not just to threaten the authority of the male God but because she was seen as threatening the Hebrew identity.

If we look at the Orthodox Jewish Bible, we find:

> And Elohim spoke unto Moshe, and said unto him, I am Hashem;
> (Hashem is used to denote the name Yahweh.) (Shemot 6:2)

These words that are attributed to Moses are the authority he uses to claim that both the kingdoms of Israel and Judah worship the same God. The clumsy patching together of very different accounts of the creation story, which we have looked at already, and of the flood, which we are about to address, can be explained by an attempt to merge two different Gods. This leads to the conclusion that the great arguments over the worship of Baal are, in fact, caused because the fiction that Yahweh and El are one God is rejected and the taunt against those who stay loyal to El is that they are traitors who worship Baal, a foreign God.

This leads to an apparent contradiction. We can say that Yahweh and El are the same God because, for many, he was and still is worshipped as one. But El remained a separate God. And yet to complicate matters further, as the name Yahweh grew in dominance, we find records of him as the husband of Asherah. Yet he appears to have maintained the character of El, less distant from his people. Irrespective of his name, it was the husband of Asherah who the women of Judah worshipped and were condemned for doing so. It was Asherah they turned to for protection. That division of gods will be explored further with an examination of the flood.

Chapter Sixteen

NOAH'S ARK

We live in a deeply cynical world. No one takes anything on trust any more. Sometimes in life, we just need to believe. We who try to interpret the world rationally are often told that we need to approach things with a gentle heart and open our minds. Well, OK, I'll try that. I'll suspend my disbelief for as long as is possible.

Millions of fundamentalists from across the three Abrahamic religions believe in the story of Noah's Ark. Here is an explanation of why from a Christian:

> As a geologist, I read in Genesis 6-9 that God subsequently judged the whole earth because of the wickedness and corruption of a rebellious mankind and a violent creation. All of mankind and every land-dwelling, air-breathing creature not in the Ark (which God had instructed Noah to build) were destroyed by the Flood waters that rose violently to eventually cover all the high hills and mountains under all the heavens (Genesis 7: 11, 17-24). And Jesus Christ, who is the Truth (John 14: 6), and so would never tell us a lie, affirmed that Noah entered the Ark and the Flood came and took them all away (Matthew 24: 37-39 and Luke 17: 26-27). He said that judgment was a warning of the judgment to come at His second coming.
>
> And when did this global Flood occur? By adding up the lifespans of the generations after the Flood from Shem to Abraham recorded in Genesis 11: 10-26, and then adding the years of the history of Abraham's descendants to the Exodus from Egypt and on to the date of the start of the building of Solomon's temple (1 Kings 6: 1), a date known archaeologically, the Flood would have occurred about 2,300-2,400 BC, or 4,300-4,400 years ago. (Andrew Snelling, Ph.D., Answers in Genesis on 6 December 2011, http://www.answersingenesis.org/articles/2011/12/06/nami-response)

If Dr Snelling doesn't melt your cold cynical heart, maybe this new evidence will. Noah's Ark has been found. And those who have found it are 99.9 per cent sure that it is Noah's Ark. That is pretty damned sure.

> A team of evangelical Christian explorers claim they've found the remains of Noah's ark beneath snow and volcanic debris on Turkey's Mount Ararat (map). (http://news.nationalgeographic.com/news/2010/04/100428-noahs-ark-found-in-turkey-science-religion-culture/)

But even as the National Geographic reported this historic find, they allowed the naysayers a voice.

> 'I don't know of any expedition that ever went looking for the ark and didn't find it,' said Paul Zimansky, an archaeologist specializing in the Middle East at Stony Brook University in New York State.

All right, so it has been found, again, but let's try to maintain our soft heart and open mind. I suppose in the interests of honesty, we might have to concede a few nit-picking points as we go along.

For a start, there is obviously a poor stitching together of stories in the account of the flood. Well, we all know the story. We have seen the cute cartoons. The animals did go into the Ark two by two. It says as much in the Bible.

> And of every living thing of all flesh, two of every sort shalt thou bring into the ark, to keep them alive with thee; they shall be male and female. (Gen. 6: 19)

The first author is identified as the Priestly author, but there is a second account identified as the author of the J text.

> Take with you seven pairs of all clean animals the male and his mate, and a pair of the animals that are not clean, the male and his mate, and seven pairs of the birds of the heavens also, male and female, to keep their offspring alive on the face of all the earth. (Gen. 7: 2-3)

Personally, I think two by two is much cuter, but there you have someone ruining the story with seven of some creatures. Don't you just hate it when a good story is complicated like that? But at least the bit about the rain, you know, it rained forty days and forty nights is true. It does say that in the Bible, after all.

> And the flood was forty days upon the earth. (Gen. 7: 17)

Well, that is as plain as plain can be. But, hold on, look what it says further down:

And the waters prevailed upon the earth an hundred and fifty days.
(Gen. 7: 24)

There the Bible goes again, ruining one of its own best stories. The two things everyone knows about the story of Noah's Ark are contradicted by itself. But hold on, none of that means the flood didn't happen. I mean, all it took was a lot of rain. Yep, we can still soft-headedly suspend our disbelief. I bet that Ark story makes perfect sense. I'm sure there are answers to the pettifogging objections. Let's start by looking at the objections.

THE ARK

HOW DID THE ANIMALS GET TO THE ARK?

1. Did penguins swim and walk all the way from Antarctica?
2. How did the Northern hairy-nosed wombats get all the way from Australia?
3. And what about the many forms of bacteria that live for less than a day?
4. How many species were on the Ark? Just to help you, the National Science Foundation's (USA) 'Tree of Life' project estimates that there could be anywhere from 5 million to 100 million species on the planet, but science has only identified about 2 million.
5. What about all the unidentified species? Did Noah go about discovering them before he built the Ark?

BUILDING THE ARK

6. What size was the Ark? Now we know the Bible, in Genesis 6: 15, helpfully gives us the dimensions of 300 cubits by 50 by 30, approximately 137 by 23 by 14 m (440 feet long, 73 feet wide, and 43 feet high). Are you absolutely certain that would have been big enough?
7. The first question is, could they even have built a seaworthy vessel of that size out of wood? How would it withstand a tsunami, many times the size of anything in recorded history?

Answers in Genesis have kindly supplied an answer.

The research team found that the proportions of Noah's Ark carefully balanced the conflicting demands of stability (resistance to capsizing), comfort ('seakeeping'), and strength. In fact, the Ark has the same proportions as a modern cargo ship.

The study also confirmed that the Ark could handle waves as high as 100 ft (30 m). Dr Hong is now director general of the facility and claims 'life came from the sea,' obviously not the words of a creationist on a mission to promote the worldwide Flood. Endorsing the seaworthiness of Noah's Ark obviously did not damage Dr Hong's credibility.

Yes, you can compare the strength of the hull of a large wooden box like the Ark to the highly skilled construction of a steel hull. If gopher wood (cypress) is the best and is just as good a material to make a large ship out of as steel, why do shipbuilders waste all that money on high-quality steel, and all that welding?

Can you provide any evidence that anyone has constructed a wooden cargo ship of that size and shown it to be seaworthy in severe weather?

Dr Hong has assessed the dimensions of that craft, but he has said nothing about the fragility of the wood in 100-foot (30 m) waves.

Gavin Pretor-Pinney in his highly informative book The Wavewatcher's Companion (2010) tells us:

> 20-30m high rogue waves have been reported for centuries by mariners amid violent storms and forming immense walls of water that are out of proportion with the other storm waves.

So, Dr Hong is only claiming a seaworthy vessel of that size could withstand condition, which, while rare, can arise in the sea in existing conditions. He is not addressing the conditions of a worldwide flood that would cover every mountain on Earth. That would be to the top of Mount Chimborazo in Ecuador. Were you thinking of Everest? That would seem to be the answer. But because of the way the Earth bulges at the equator, it turns out to be Mount Chimborazo. The important thing is that it would not be Mount Arafat. The boat would have to have sunk to have ended up there before any other peak had appeared.

THE WATER

1. Even if we go with the longer time range of rain falling at a steady pace of over a 150 days, we are looking at a rate of 88 inches (2 m 23.5 cm) an hour or 176 feet (approximately 54 m) a day. If we work on the calculation of the Earth flooding to cover the mountain tops over a period of forty days, we need an average rate of water rise of 27.5 feet (approximately 8.5 m) an hour. All the rivers, seas, and oceans would rush into each other, and the world would become one big ocean. Now all Creationists need to do is explain in a coherent manner how any vessel could survive that especially when we consider the cargo it would be carrying.

2.   All the waterfalls in the world would be overflowing at many times the rate of anything in recorded history. Every mountain top and every cliff would become a torrent. The power of the water would sweep buildings, trees, and everything along. There would be landslides of rocks. There would be such power in the force of the water that it would cause the process known as liquefaction, where soil becomes liquid, and trees and rubble are swept along. All of that would either sink down into the sea or float. Wood floats, and even Creationists have to admit trees are made of wood; massive forests of trees would float. They would float as fast as the Ark. As the rivers and seas rose into the oceans and the oceans merged into one ocean, how would the Ark have avoided colliding with the floating forest?

3.   The evidence of that catastrophe would be all over the world. We would still be able to find it. Why don't we have a geological record?

4.   Why is this version of the flood not mentioned in the annals of China from about 1700 BCE. They do have a flood myth, but in it a brother and sister survive, get married, and have a baby without arms or legs, which the brother cut into small pieces. The pieces turned into people and repopulated the world (http://www.pitt.edu/~dash/chinaflood.html).

5.   If the world had been flooded, about 500 years before, in the complete way mentioned in the Bible, surely, it would have been as much a part of their history as of the Israelites. Why do they omit to mention it?

6.   Since we are on the topic of China, how come the world was repopulated enough to have large and very diverse civilisation all over the globe in just 500 years, and all from the descendants of Noah?

THE ANIMALS ON THE ARK

7.   How would the Ark have withstood the weight of all those live animals and their food, not to mention the waste they produced? A male lion eats 7 kg (15 lb) of food per day, a female slightly less 5 kg (11 lb). The time on the Ark is about 375 days in total, 9,750 lb in a year, about 4,423 kg just for a pair of lions. A pair of tigers will eat approximately 77 lb (35 kg) of meat a day. All I want Creationist to provide are the estimates for the amount of food the Ark would have needed to carry.

8.   How much would that have added to the weight of the Ark?

9.   How did Noah keep that meat fresh? Was there a bank of Bronze Age freezers which archaeologists have yet to discover?

10. What would Noah have done about bacteria that live for less than a day? How would he have fed them? What did he do about parasites? Did he ensure they had a host to live on?

11. What would he have done about feeding the animals after the flood? The whole landscape of the world would have been laid waste. Vegetation would have been destroyed.

12. Since all the animals had been wiped out, there would be no prey for lions and tigers once they had been set free form the Ark. What would they eat? Hold on, they could, of course, eat the pair of deer and the goats Noah had so carefully preserved. Well, if they wanted to survive, they'd have to. So how did the only two deer in the world survive when lions and tigers had nothing else to eat? (Do you know Answers in Genesis has no answer to that? It doesn't even seem to have considered the problem.)

THE SEARCH FOR THE ARK

1. How come the search for Noah's Ark centres in the Mediterranean, in places like Mount Arafat? If the Noah's Ark story had been true and Earth flooded to mountain tops, the Ark would have landed on the highest point. As we have established due to the way the Earth bulges at the equator that is Mount Chimborazo in Ecuador. Failing that the next best possibility would be Mount Everest but not Turkey. Mount Arafat would have been deeply submerged.

2. You would almost think Moses didn't realise the world beyond the Mediterranean existed, when he supposedly wrote his account of the flood. My question to Creationists is, have you any evidence God had yet heard of the American or Australian continents?

Well, all the soft-heartedness and being open-minded in the world wouldn't make the story of Noah's Ark make sense to me. It is a myth, and no more.

THE MAINSTREAM CHRISTIAN APPROACH

If you are a mainstream Christian, you may well have found yourself in agreement with my account of Noah's Ark. You may agree that it is an absurd idea. But I have a point for you to consider. Noah's Ark is not even the most absurd idea in the Bible. Here are some questions to consider.

What is the rational basis for not accepting the Noah's Ark story but still accepting the miracles of Jesus, the virgin birth, and the resurrection story? Why reject one irrational claim but still accept others? Noah's Ark makes no sense because it defied the laws of physics and what we know about nature. Don't the miracles of Jesus do the same?

How the Jesus Story

was invented.

Chapter Seventeen

JESUS AND HOW THE BIBLE WAS MADE

For God so loved the world, that he gave his only begotten Son, that
whosoever believeth in him should not perish, but have everlasting life.
(John 3: 16, KJV)

This is one of the most popular Bible quotations that Christians use when
proclaiming how loving God is. It is worth first considering the word 'begotten'. If
Jesus was God and God is eternal, we might as well ask how he could have been
'begotten'? That implies that Jesus who is supposed to be part or the eternal God
needed a progenitor. That is far from the only problem with this idea.

God, the Father, is supposedly omnipotent and omniscient, so even before he
begot Jesus, he knew everything that would happen to him. He knew about his birth
and childhood, he knew how he would grow up, and everything he would say and do
in his life of teaching. Most important of all, he knew about his arrest, trial, and slow
torturous death on the cross. It was God's choice to allow this to happen. The only
conclusion we can draw is that God created Jesus for the purpose of being sacrificed.
Is that a good example of parental love?

There will, of course, be those who argue that sacrifice is sometimes necessary.
They have a case. If there had been no sacrifice to stop Hitler, the world would have
been indescribably worse than it is. However, there is a big difference between the
necessary sacrifice to defeat Hitler and the death of Christ. Those who fought against
the Nazis didn't create the world. It is, however, claimed that the God of the Bible did.

We have been through the argument before when addressing the idea of an
all-loving, all-powerful, and all-knowing God. The point remains the same: Jesus is
sent to solve a problem which an all-powerful God could have avoided in the first
place. He is portrayed as being sent to save humanity when it makes as much sense to
say he was sent to create a justification for God creating a suffering world.

That is, after all, what the whole Jesus story is about. It glorifies suffering. Before we even get to the crucifixion, we get the repeated message that suffering is worthwhile and will lead to an eventual reward. The Beatitudes are often set up as most perfect of moral teaching and the truest example of God's love. It is hard to think of anything in literature which is so steeped in such a misplaced and ill-thought through sentimentality. We need to get past that sentimentality and look at them to see what they are actually saying.

> Blessed are the poor in spirit,
>> For theirs is the kingdom of heaven.
> Blessed are those who mourn,
>> For they shall be comforted.
> Blessed are the meek,
>> For they shall inherit the earth.
> Blessed are those who hunger and thirst for righteousness,
>> For they shall be filled.
> Blessed are the merciful,
>> For they shall obtain mercy.
> Blessed are the pure in heart,
>> For they shall see God.
> Blessed are the peacemakers,
>> For they shall be called sons of God.
> Blessed are those who are persecuted for righteousness' sake,
>> For theirs is the kingdom of heaven.

> Blessed are you when they revile and persecute you, and say all kinds of evil against you falsely for My sake. Rejoice and be exceedingly glad, for great is your reward in heaven, for so they persecuted the prophets who were before you. (Matt. 5: 3-12)

Let's sum up what the Beatitudes actually say in one line: it will be all right when you are dead. The essence of the message is, endure suffering now and you will be rewarded in Heaven. If you are feeling down and poor in spirit being told, you'll be OK in Heaven isn't exactly comforting.

They promise that the mourning will be comforted. Well, that is great, just a shame that they will have to be dead first. You might think I am misinterpreting that, and it means that Jesus will comfort the suffering in this life. Religion is, after all, often claimed to be a comfort at such time. One of the few organisations to investigate this issue has been The National Cancer Institute, based in Maryland; they say:

> . . . empirical results about the benefits of religion in coping with death tend to be mixed, some showing positive benefit and others

showing no benefit or even greater distress among the religious. (http://www.cancer.gov/cancertopics/pdq/supportivecare/bereavement/HealthProfessional/page1/AllPages#Section_216)

Oh, well, maybe Jesus was right about the meek inheriting the Earth? I once pointed out to a believer that there wasn't any sign of that. He helpfully suggested that it means in the last days. I said that the Earth as described in The Revelation of John is not an inheritance I'd wish on anyone. And there is no sign that the merciful receive mercy. As for the pure in heart, peacemakers, and those persecuted for righteousness, their rewards are vague, too.

Ah, but the point of all this is then revealed to us. Being persecuted for Jesus will bring you a great reward in Heaven. All that suffering is a means of pointing out how important Jesus is. The point of life is to serve Jesus. How is that anything but egomania? That egomania contradicts the claims of spirituality which emphasise humility. I can well imagine believers who read this are offended, but that is not my intention. I am seriously asking you how, that differs from the narcissism of a man like David Koresh? Koresh led the Branch Davidians religious sect in Waco, Texas. It was very much a personality cult and ended after a stand-off with the Bureau of Alcohol, Tobacco and Firearms (ATF) when the camp caught fire during a raid by the FBI. Koresh saw himself as the second coming of Christ.

Christ's message was continually about how important he was and demanding dependency on him. The only difference lies in belief. If you believe the Jesus's myth, you will interpret everything in that light. Sadly, both the Jesus and Koresh myths led to violent death.

There is an argument between two non-believing and highly able academics over the question of whether or not Jesus ever existed. Bart Erhman argues that there is sufficient evidence to say that while many of the claims about Jesus are not true, a first century rabbi who was the founding figure of Christianity did exist. Richard Carrier argues that there was no need for such a figure, that revelation was the most important factor. He points to Paul writing:

> But I make known to you, brethren, that the gospel which was preached by me is not according to man. For I neither received it from man, nor was I taught it, but it came through the revelation of Jesus Christ. (Gal. 1: 11-12)

Biblical scholars don't agree which of the books of the New Testament was written first. However, Carrier and Erhman and most serious biblical scholars agree that the earliest were some of the Epistles of Paul. The most likely candidates are The First Epistle to the Thessalonians and The Epistle to the Galatians. Galatians is said by some sources to have been published as early as the year 49 CE (or AD 49).

Paul's claims about Christ are certainly not initially founded on a direct knowledge from the disciples. He tells us that his understanding is not based on any experience of the world but from a direct spiritual experience.

Carrier, in an argument classed as mythicism, therefore argues that Jesus was created out of visions and the stories about the supposed real man came later. There is certainly a case to be made for the Jesus of the gospels being influenced by Paul. However, Erhman argues that that does not mean there was no man on whom the Jesus story was based. He also uses the Book of Galatians to support his claim.

> Then after three years I went up to Jerusalem to see Peter, and remained with him fifteen days. But I saw none of the other apostles except James, the Lord's brother. (Gal. 1: 18-19)

Erhman argues that Paul knew James, and James ought to have known who his own brother was. That would appear to be game, set and match to Erhman, except we are left with the intriguing possibility that one of the many transcribers of the Pauline letters spotted the name James, affixed a note that he was the brother of Jesus, and that note became part of the epistle. The sort of thing certainly did happen. And so they wrangle on.

If you really want to pursue this:

Richard Carrier puts his case on http://www.youtube.com/watch?v=mwUZOZN-9dc
Bart Erhman puts his case on http://www.youtube.com/watch?v=eV9JVEtDS8E

Richard Dawkins has on more than one occasion stated that it doesn't matter much whether there was, or not, an historical figure called Jesus. His point is that if there was such a figure, his existence would not be evidence that any of the extraordinary claims about him were true. However, it does create an interesting problem for believers and, in particular, for how Christianity was to develop. To understand that, we need to first understand how the Bible was created.

Anyone who has read The Da Vinci Code, or seen the film, will know that the question of which books would be included into the Bible was settled in 325 CE, at the Council of Nicea, under the watchful eye of Constantine the Great. Anyone who has actually looked at the history, of the period, will know that Dan Brown wrote his book based on a very weak grasp of the historical facts. Versions of the canon had been around for a long time. Marcion of Sinope (ca 85-160), who was branded a heretic for claiming the God of the Old and New Testaments were different gods (now that is an enduring heresy), is said to have compiled one of the earliest. There were rival versions. However, the canon, as we recognise it, was not established, by any formal body, until nearly seventy years after Nicea, at the Council of Hippo in 393 CE. The first definitive Bible was not produced until the year 400. Even then its contents were not rigidly set. At the Council of Trent in response to the Reformation, the Catholic Church decreed precisely what the scriptures were in 1546. Five of those books were dropped, from it, by those compiling the Bible for Protestants.

The Protestant Bible, from the King James to the modern versions that lose all the poetry, has sixty-six books, and the Catholic Bible has seventy-one books, but there are more books that didn't make it into either canon. There is the Infancy Gospel of Thomas (found in The Lost Books of the Bible, Testament Books, 1979), where a very dark tale of the childhood of Jesus is told. The young Jesus curses a boy, who upsets him, and causes him to fall dead. When the dead boy's parents understandably complain to Jesus's parents, they are struck blind. Anyone who has seen the horror film The Omen will immediately spot what, at least, some of the plotline was based on.

The name Thomas is used pseudonymously (a name attributed falsely to a work). It is also used for a very different non-canonical work the Gospel of Thomas, which is found in The Nag Hammadi Scriptures (2008). This is a collection of sayings which are attributed to Jesus. Many are versions of sayings found in the New Testament, but there are many additional ones not found there. The Nag Hammadi Scriptures are a collection of thirteen papyrus codices, meaning books rather than scrolls, which were buried in large jars, in Upper Egypt, in the second half of the fourth century. They were rediscovered in 1947, and each book contained a number of non-canonical 'Gnostic' writings. They added to the non-canonical scriptures that had already been known.

So the first problem with the Bible is, if Christians' claim it is the word of God, how do they decide what should be included in it? Protestants and Catholics don't agree, and there are a number of books, which both have excluded, that have as strong a claim to validity as the existing canon. There is the Gospel of Thomas that is mentioned above. There is also the Revelation of Peter which was seen as canonical by many early Christians and is included in the Muratorian Fragment, the oldest surviving list of New Testament books but was rejected to make room for the more dramatic the Revelation of John. The version attributed to John certainly has more literary merit. Anyone who likes a good horror movie must agree. The Revelation of John has inspired countless horror stories and films. The Revelation of Peter might just about inspire a vicar's tea party. That suggests that the decision on which books survived in the canon was, at least sometimes, based more on an ongoing Pulitzer Prize process than any attempt at divine inspiration.

The important thing to understand about the canon is that the books were not ordered according to the dates when they were written. Books were revised and amalgamated. The Book of Isaiah is believed to have been written by three different authors over more than a couple of hundred years. The authorship and the order in which books were written matters. An earlier book can influence a later one. That matters if we are to understand how beliefs developed.

So if instead of reading the New Testament in the order the books are presented to us in the Bible, we read them in the order in which the books appear to have been written in, we will find the New Testament to be a very different book. That, of course, is not always easy, as it is very difficult to precisely date when any of the books were written. Instead of starting with The Gospel According to St. Matthew, with that very odd genealogy showing Jesus was descended from King David, we start with the book that was written first. Conservative Christians who believe in Bible inerrancy argue that the Bible was written in the order presented. Most Bible scholars argue that the books are not in a chronological order. When it comes to the New Testament, the prevailing view is the earliest were 1 Thessalonians and Galatians. However, that does not answer the question of authorship.

Most scholars agree that Paul wrote Romans 1 and 2, Corinthians, Philemon, Galatians, Philippians, and 1 Thessalonians. Colossians was probably written by Paul, and 2 Thessalonians and Ephesians were possibly written by him. 1 and 2 Timothy and Titus were pseudonymous. Together, they form the majority of the New Testament. Richard Carrier (in the link above) points out that the seven books attributed to Paul are the books in the Bible for which there is most certainty over the authorship. Jesus may or may not have existed, but the author of these letters who called himself by the name of Saul or Paul certainly did.

If there was a real man called Jesus, his name would have been Yeshua. Yeshua would have been a religious leader at a time when Judaism was fragmented into many groups. There'd have been the Pharisees, Sadducees, Herodians, Essenes, and Zealots amongst others. His arguments with some of these groups are found throughout the gospels. The Dead Sea Scrolls authors would have claimed him as an Essene. Well, they would, wouldn't they? He may have been some kind of non-aligned rabbi. Whatever he was, he certainly appears to have upset the temple authorities with a bit of violent direct action against moneylenders. There is nothing non-violent about charging round a place of worship attacking people with a whip, after all. It is hardly surprising he ended up being executed. These claims are all entirely consistent with being human. No one would need to believe anything supernatural to accept claims like that. These are claims about a man called Yeshua.

Paul is not making claims about a man called Yeshua. He makes it very clear that his claims come from no man. Paul is making claims about an encounter with a vision. Yeshua is a man; the Jesus Paul claims to speak on behalf of is a product of his own mental experience. Think about it. If someone came up to you and announced they'd just had a vision of Jesus and he'd told them all sorts of things, would you think 'I've been waiting all my life for this.' Or would you try to get away from them as fast as you could?

The words of Paul are read unquestioningly in churches, but it is worth looking at what is going on in them. The Book of Galatians is the account of the life of a leading member of a cult that had been formed in recent years. There is a rift over the treatment of non-Jewish, specifically non-circumcised members of the cult. Paul is behaving like someone who is seeking to gain control of it and is not afraid to attack his opponents.

> But when Peter came to Antioch, I withstood him to his face, because he was to be blamed. For before certain ones came from James, he ate with the Gentiles; but when they had come, he withdrew and separated himself from them, fearing those who were of the Circumcision. And the other Jews dissembled likewise with him, so much that Barnabas also was carried away by their dissimulation. But when I saw that they walked not uprightly according to the truth of the Gospel, I said unto Peter before them all, If thou, being a Jew, livest after the manner of Gentiles and not as do the Jews, why compellest thou the Gentiles to live as do the Jews? (Gal. 2: 11-14)

This is an unashamed attempt to rest the leadership of the cult from Peter and assert Paul's moral authority. The message is stark. Peter might have been the close companion of Jesus, but Paul's visions gave him the greater moral position.

All the claims we know about the life of Jesus were written after this account by Paul. There is passion in Paul's writing. We could even say that he sometimes ranted:

> O foolish Galatians! Who hath bewitched you, that you should not obey the truth, before whose eyes Jesus Christ hath been clearly set forth, crucified among you? (Gal. 3: 1)

We find more ranting:

> Now the works of the flesh are manifest, and they are these: adultery, fornication, uncleanness, lasciviousness, Idolatry, witchcraft, hatred, quarreling, rivalry, wrath, strife, seditions, heresies, Envying, murders, drunkenness, revelings, and such like. About these things I tell you again, as I have also told you in times past, that those who do such things shall not inherit the Kingdom of God. (Gal. 5: 19-21)

What is unmistakeable is that Paul was intent on imposing his understanding on this new movement however we find an opposing view in the Book of James.

> What does it profit, my brethren, if someone says he has faith but does not have works? Can faith save him? If a brother or sister is naked and destitute of daily food, And one of you says to them, 'Depart in peace, be warmed and filled,' but you do not give them the things which are needed for the body, what does it profit? Thus also faith by itself, if it does not have works, is dead. (Jas. 2: 14-17)

However, Paul writes:

> And if by grace, then it is no longer of works; otherwise grace is no longer grace. But if it is of works, it is no longer grace; otherwise work is no longer work. (Rom. 11: 6)

This is an argument that echoes down the ages. Paul rejects James's emphasis on works and declares that grace is what matters. His inspiration came from grace. God has changed him. He has got Jesus in his life and in his heart, and he wasted no time in letting everyone know it. Truth comes from that direct revelation. He claims that life after death and the religious cult, for it is no more at that stage, are the property of those who have had the truth revealed to them. There is an important question over how Paul constructed the image of Christ. When he writes:

> And if there is any other commandment, are all summed up in this saying, namely, 'You shall love your neighbor as yourself.' Love does no harm to a neighbor; therefore love is the fulfillment of the law. (Rom. 13:9-10)

He is referring to the Law of Moses. That is what the phrase 'fulfilment of the law' means. The phrase has its origins in the Book of Leviticus.

> You shall not take vengeance, nor bear any grudge against the children of your people, but you shall love your neighbor as yourself: I am the Lord. (Lev. 19: 18)

Paul relates these words to the commandments as explained in that book. He links the role of Christ to the end of time. He was not writing for the distant future; he was doing the equivalent of going round with a sandwich board that declared 'The End is Nigh'.

> This, knowing the time, that now it is high time to awake out of sleep; for now our salvation is nearer And do than when we first believed. (Rom. 13: 11)

He is convinced that the world will end in the lifetime of some of those he addresses.

> For the Lord himself shall descend from heaven with a shout, with the voice of the archangel, and with the trump of God: and the dead in Christ shall rise first: Then we which are alive and remain shall be caught up together with them in the clouds, to meet the Lord in the air: and so shall we ever be with the Lord. (1 Thess. 4: 16-17)

It would not be fair to compare Paul to Harold Camping for two reasons. Harold Camping predicted the end of the world in September 1994 and again predicted 'the first day of the Day of Judgment' would be on 21 May 2011, and the world would end on 21 October 2011. Paul does not appear to have been so precise in his prediction, and nor is there any evidence that his ministry made him into a very wealthy man. But both men gathered many followers around their prediction that the end was at hand.

For Paul, death is the focus of all things. It is where he seeks his glory.

> And why stand we in jeopardy every hour? I protest by your rejoicing which I have in Christ Jesus our Lord, I die daily. If after the manner of men I have fought with beasts at Ephesus, what advantageth it me, if the dead rise not? let us eat and drink; for tomorrow we die. (1 Cor. 15:30-32)

There is a deep sense of self-importance in this attitude. The tragic and forsaken lover declares, 'Without you my world is over.' Compared to Paul or Camping, this is a weak and half-hearted sentiment. For they declare, 'When I die, the universe ends.' It appears to be an incapacity to conceive how the universe could possibly go on without them.

Whether or not there ever was a first-century rabbi upon whom the myth of Jesus was based is truly inconsequential. It was Paul who shaped the myth. Paul himself becomes a myth. Others followed and borrowed from Paul's swings from rhapsodies on love to dark predictions. Ask most Christians what the main theme of the New Testament is, and they will tell you Love. A close examination of it brings up a very different result.

Chapter Eighteen

HELL

There are two main schools of Christian thought on Hell. The first, which you find in many evangelicals, always reminds me of the words of a song from the 1969 musical Oh What a lovely war!

> The Bells of Hell go ting-a-ling-a-ling
> For you but not for me:
> For me the angels sing-a-ling-a-ling,
> They've got the goods for me.
> Oh! Death, where is thy sting-a-ling-a-ling?
> Oh! Grave, where is thy victory?
> The Bells of Hell go ting-a-ling-a-ling
> For you but not for me.

In the film, it is sung after the burial of dead soldiers and is part of the condemnation of the futility of the First World War, yet it also reflects the attitude of those who gleefully think they are saved by their 'true faith', while the rest of humanity will find a terrible fate in eternity. Of course, this attitude is often expressed with a thin pretence of concern.

I've been told 'I'm just worried what you'll say when you are dead.' However, sometimes it is more direct and brutal. I've been told 'You'll be sorry when you get to the afterlife! What will you have to say for yourself?' Yes, it is wonderful how, when believers have no answers to non-believers' arguments, they often proclaim how they will be proved right in eternity. It always seems like a desperate tactic when the only way they can claim to snatch victory is to claim the argument will be resolved by eternal damnation.

One line we often come across is that Hell is a matter of free will. Well, if it is free will, when did each of us make that choice? Did we choose to be born? Did we choose a world in which there is no evidence for God? Did we choose the religion of our parents and community? When did we sign a contract that would lead to Hell if we defaulted? How is the idea that either you comply with the will of God or you go to Hell a free choice? Surely, it is the choice of a slave. Either we obey or are punished. If God is all powerful, he knowingly ordained things that way.

There is another response to Hell, that of the Liberal Christians. To be frank, most Liberal Christians are pretty embarrassed by the whole idea of Hell. When I have raised the topic with them, they have argued it is essentially an Old Testament idea or that you will find it only in the Book of Revelations (note that is their 's' not mine). It is the Book of the Revelation of Saint John the Divine or the Apocalypse of John or the Book of Revelation, for short. They'll argue that this book isn't something anyone would take seriously, unless they are an evangelical or shouting about God on a street corner. The point is it doesn't fit with their cosy and cuddly image of Jesus, who didn't go round talking about Hell all the time.

There is only one thing wrong with this viewpoint. It is wrong. It is not the Old Testament but the New Testament that dwells on eternal damnation. The Book of Revelation is not concerned with Hell but with the end of the world, and the terrible events it predicts come from Heaven not Hell. It does mention Hell but only three times. So it does not tell us much about Christianity's attitude towards Hell. For that you need to read the first book of the New Testament and not the just the last book.

The first book of the New Testament is, of course, the Gospel According to St. Matthew. There you will find reference after reference to Hell hiding in plain sight. If you want to avoid them, don't read the book. They are found at the very heart of the teachings of Jesus. Try chapter seven:

> Every tree that bringeth not forth good fruit is hewn down, and cast into the fire. Wherefore by their fruits ye shall know them. Not every one that saith unto me, Lord, Lord, shall enter into the kingdom of heaven; but he that doeth the will of my Father which is in heaven. (Matt. 7: 19-21)

It is a statement of what Christopher Hitchens loved to call the 'celestial dictatorship'. Heaven is only accessible to those who submit to the Lord. As for the rest, they are cast down into the fire. Even if they plead and cry out in the name of the Lord, it will do them no good. In chapter eight, we get some of the most memorable imagery of Hell.

> But the children of the kingdom shall be cast out into outer darkness: there shall be weeping and gnashing of teeth. (Matt. 8: 12)

The author of The Gospel According to St. Matthew did like his metaphors for suffering. As unpleasant as the outer darkness would be, it would be better than burning eternally in the flames. I think we can assume that there are no dentists in Hell. Well, none who are allowed to practise there. Maybe eternal untreated toothache is, after all, a worse punishment. I'd guess Hell doesn't have anywhere you can pop into to grab a pack of analgesics and being in the dark, where all you could hear was all that gnashing of teeth, would get pretty irritating. Frankly, the mental torture would be unbearable.

There is absolutely no compassion for anyone who rejects the message and not just individuals. If a town doesn't rush out and greet the word of the Lord with open arms, everyone in it will face a terrible fate.

> And whosoever shall not receive you, nor hear your words, when ye depart out of that house or city, shake off the dust of your feet. Verily I say unto you, It shall be more tolerable for the land of Sodom and Gomorrah in the day of judgment, than for that city. (Matt. 10: 14-15)

The fate of Sodom and Gomorrah was so terrible that Lot's wife was turned into a pillar of salt just for looking at it. Well, it might be preferable to be turned into a pillar of salt than either of those alternatives.

> And fear not them which kill the body, but are not able to kill the soul: but rather fear him which is able to destroy both soul and body in hell. (Matt. 10: 28)

So apparently, Hell is both physical and mental torment. I know there are plenty of well-meaning liberal-minded Christians who try and claim that Hell is just 'absence from God'. They will cheerfully explain that those of us who fail the entrance exam for Heaven are put in to some benign celestial outer room, but that is most certainly not what it says in the New Testament. Chapter eleven leaves us in no doubt. How he waxes lyrical:

> But to what will I compare this generation? It is like children sitting in the marketplaces and calling to one another, We played the flute for you, and you did not dance; we wailed, and you did not mourn. For John came neither eating nor drinking, and they say, 'He has a demon'; The Son of Man came eating and drinking, and they say, 'Look, a glutton and a drunkard, a friend of tax collectors and sinners!' Yet wisdom is vindicated by her deeds. Then he began to reproach the cities in which most of his deeds of power had been done, because they did not repent. Woe to you, Chorazin! Woe to you, Bethsaida! For if the deeds of power done in you had been done in Tyre and Sidon, they would have repented long ago

in sackcloth and ashes. But I tell you, on the day of judgment it will be more tolerable for Tyre and Sidon than for you. And you, Capernaum, will you be exalted to heaven? No, you will be brought down to Hades. For if the deeds of power done in you had been done in Sodom, it would have remained until this day. But I tell you that on the day of judgment it will be more tolerable for the land of Sodom than for you. (Matt. 11: 16-24)

The truth is that Christians are often so used to their religion that they never stand back from it to see how dark a religion it is. It is a religion which has death, damnation, and blood sacrifice at the heart of it.

Chapter Nineteen

BLOOD SACRIFICE

By the time we come to the First Epistle of Peter, believed to have been written about the year 81, in the reign of the Emperor Domitian, the pages are virtually dripping blood.

> Elect according to the foreknowledge of God the Father, through sanctification of the Spirit, unto obedience and sprinkling of the blood of Jesus Christ: Grace unto you, and peace, be multiplied.

And

> But with the precious blood of Christ, as of a lamb without blemish and without spot: (1 Pet. 1: 2, 19)

In the origins of all the Abrahamic traditions lies the idea of a God who demanded blood sacrifices, who regarded killing as a sacred act. We find a particularly graphic account of this when Moses ordains Aaron and his sons.

> And he brought the bullock for the sin offering: and Aaron and his sons laid their hands upon the head of the bullock for the sin offering. And he slew it; and Moses took the blood, and put it upon the horns of the altar round about with his finger, and purified the altar, and poured the blood at the bottom of the altar, and sanctified it, to make reconciliation upon it. And he took all the fat that was upon the inwards, and the caul above the liver, and the two kidneys, and their fat, and Moses burned it upon the altar. But the bullock, and his hide, his flesh, and his dung, he burnt with fire without the camp; as the Lord commanded Moses. (Lev. 8: 14-17)

A ram and a bullock, beasts of great value, are slaughtered as part of the most sacred of sacred acts. This is done alongside very lavish offerings of gold. The altar is purified with blood. Would you want to go into a butcher's shop (if you go into butcher's shops) with blood all over the walls? Would you consider that a sacred space? Yet we are told Moses, believed by many to be the great lawgiver, considered something similar to it to be sacred. It is there we find the origins of the grotesque myth of a man dying a slow torturous death while nailed to one or a couple of pieces of wood being sacred. There is no evidence of a cross being as it is portrayed today. It may have been one stake or a T-shape. Whatever the implement of death, it is a savage fantasy of death. The idea that humanity was saved by the slow, ugly, and torturous death of a man nailed to a wooden structure is frankly obscene.

QUR'AN

Islam does not see the blood of an animal as a direct sacrifice to God, but it does have a tradition of a festival of sacrifice (Eid al-Adha) when wealthy affluent Muslims all over the world perform the Sunnah of Prophet Ibrahim (Abraham) by having a cow or sheep sacrificed. The meat is then equally divided with the person who performs the sacrifice, his relatives, and the poor. The Qur'an states that the sacrifice is not one of blood and gore to God.

> It is not their meat nor their blood that reaches God. It is your piety
> that reaches Him . . . (Surah 22: 37)

This reflects the fact that the Qur'an was written in the early medieval period when blood sacrifices were no longer an accepted practice. However, the sacrifice at Eid does recall Abraham appeasing God with the blood of a ram, in the place of his son Isaac. Aaron is regarded, in Islam, as the brother of Moses and therefore a highly respected prophet. So Islam has an origin as steeped in the blood of animal sacrifice as either Christianity or Judaism.

Chapter Twenty

THE PROBLEM OF EVIL

> So whom does God wrong in commanding the destruction of the Canaanites? Not the Canaanite adults, for they were corrupt and deserving of judgment. Not the children, for they inherit eternal life. So who is wronged? Ironically, I think the most difficult part of this whole debate is the apparent wrong done to the Israeli soldiers themselves. Can you imagine what it would be like to have to break into some house and kill a terrified woman and her children? The brutalising effect on these Israeli soldiers is disturbing. (William Lane Craig, http://www.goodreads.com/author/quotes/72189.William_Lane_Craig)

Let's be clear about what William Lane Craig, a prominent Christian apologist, is saying. The killing of men, women, and children, what could be described as an act of genocide, is justified if you believe God has instructed you to do it. It is the justification of the cruellest of psychopathic killers down the ages.

'God told me to do it.' Is at the heart of the case Lane Craig makes. It is a very simple moral position. That is whatever God does or instructs cannot be evil. It can't be so because God is the intrinsic source of all that is good.

Lane Craig claims to base his argument on the following philosophical position in The Kalām Cosmological Argument:

1. Everything that begins to exist has a cause of its existence.
2. The universe began to exist.
3. Therefore, the universe has a cause of its existence.

He concludes that therefore God exists, and God, as the creator of the universe, is supremely good. The simple answer is that while it is often supposed that everything has a beginning that has not been proven. A multi-verse theory may open up the possibility of existence going back for eternity. Lane Craig can't provide any more actual evidence for God than I can for that. However, I'm prepared to concede I don't know the origins of the universe, which is a more reasonable position than the one he takes.

You might well be asking what an explanation for the beginning of the universe has to do with genocide. It is, indeed, an extraordinary leap of illogic. To seek out such a philosophical explanation demonstrates the length people will go to in order to justify a belief. For Lane Craig, his belief is the measure and moral arbiter of all things. He believes in a supremely loving God, and that belief shapes his world.

His morality amounts to loyalty to God. Yet to command genocide is the worst of tyranny. Lane Craig defends that charge on the grounds that God, whom he claims is the founder of the universe, can do no wrong. It is no more than the old myth that the king can do no wrong. But he justifies it with the claim that God's law is the only objective morality.

The first problem with Lane Craig's argument is that he has what we have already seen is a very poor justification for the existence of God. His second is that he has used it to justify terrible actions that can be objectively shown to be evil. That objective test is unjustified harm to other humans. By any standard, killing people is harm. That could be justified on the grounds of needing to defend yourself or others. That does not apply here. The slaughter of the Canaanites was justified by the belief that God commanded it. It is justified, therefore, on the basis of belief. If Lane Craig is arguing that belief, and in particular, belief in God, justices killing, he has no grounds to condemn the 9/11 bombers. They appear to have acted on precisely the same justification as those who attacked the Canaanites.

Lane Craig will dispute my right to declare that unjustified harm is a test of what is wrong. His assertion is that humans have no right to decide on morality. That is the preserve of God. He claims if there is a moral law, there has to be a moral lawgiver, and he argues that morality is evidence of God. But this implies that we as humans are unable to decide moral questions for ourselves. If that were so, many questions before legislatures could not be decided on, and judges could not rule on many cases unless Lane Craig is claiming that political and judicial decisions arise directly from divine guidance.

But he has no evidence for that God. He only has a weak philosophical claim. I, on the other hand, have the evidence that every society on Earth, irrespective of their religious position, has an ethic against unjustified harm. That moral position is the property of humanity and not of any religion. Lane Craig is asserting that morality can only be based on a belief in God. However, he is contradicted by the evidence that a moral sense does not appear to be confined to humans alone.

Animals, particularly those that live in groups, have rules of behaviour. The only difference between that and human morality is that animals can't articulate or legislate for those rules. The argument that we are in some way morally superior to animals, which many believers make, is worth examining. An interesting study has been made on the difference in the way penguins and ravens differ in their attitude towards theft.

> Ethologist Marc Bekoff has observed thieving penguins in the wild and did not get the sense that they knew stealing stones was wrong. Ravens who steal food, on the other hand, do know they're misbehaving, Bekoff said. The distinction arises from the different way that ravens' and penguins' peers react to the thievery.
>
> 'In the raven situation, their social organization depends on treating each other fairly and not stealing, so they punish animals that have stolen food and treat them different from ones that haven't. In the penguin situation, they don't do that. Penguins that steal are not ostracized by their group,' he said. Thus there's no moral code of conduct being violated in the case of the penguins, and in the video, the thief steals stealthily not because it thinks its actions are wrong, but rather because that's simply the best way to get its neighbor's stones, he explained. (Live Science, 1 November 2011, http://news.yahoo.com/animals-know-wrong-clues-point-yes-150408317.html)

So we are faced with a simple question: why do ravens police against theft while penguins don't? Did a creator or evolution arbitrarily grant a moral sense to ravens but not penguins? Well, since evolution does not do anything intentionally, but is a question of adaption to the environment, we can only say these differences arise out of the needs of each species. Each follows the best strategy for the survival of the species.

> 'The little we know now about the moral behaviour of animals really leads us to conclude that it's much more developed than we previously gave them credit for,' Bekoff said. 'We are not the sole occupants of the moral arena—and it's unlikely that we would be, given what we know about evolution.' (Live Science, 1 November 2011, http://news.yahoo.com/animals-know-wrong-clues-point-yes-150408317.html)

If the moral code of birds is a question of adaption to environment, where is the argument that human morality evolved for any other reason? After all, a society without sanctions against murder or theft would not survive for long. It, therefore, makes more sense to say that religion arose from the primitive need to assert a code of morality rather than to claim morality arises from religion. Religion was, at least in part, a primitive attempt to enforce morality and that remains one of its primary functions today. However, democratic societies, with functioning legislators, can now decide on major questions of harm. Lesser matters are, in effect, decided within human relationships. We have also evolved characteristics such as empathy which cause us to feel concern for others. We don't need a religious faith to feel empathy.

Empathy is an essential human characteristic. Our survival is often dependant on the survival of groups rather than just the individual, and protection of the group is often the most powerful instinct across species. The dog that defends its attacked owner does not do so to ensure the survival of its genes but to protect a member of its group. The pet dog is a wolf which has adapted to live in a human environment and become a member of a human/canine group.

As we have already addressed, identification with the group is the primary cause of religious violence. It is hard to see how William Lane Craig is doing any more than defending the interests of the religious group he identifies with. The three Abrahamic religions claim they have one thing, in common, that shows they are based on divine guidance. That is the Ten Commandments which came directly from God.

It is a puzzle as to why the Ten Commandments are held up as the ultimate code and source of morality. For a start, you'd think something so important would be clear and unambiguous. Yet in the Bible, there are two different versions in Exodus 20:1-17 and Deuteronomy 5:4-21, and these lead to different Jewish, Protestant, Catholic, and Islamic versions.

The first three or four commandments (depending on the version) all address the vanity of the deity. They state 'I am' the Lord God who has led you out of Egypt and you must have no other gods before you.' So how does this apply to those of us not lead out of Egypt and what is that reference to other gods? Note it doesn't say imaginary gods. It says other gods. Now believers will claim it means things like sex or money, but if these are a straightforward set of laws, why does it not say that? After all, the tenth commandment doesn't shy away from listing exactly what it means when it comes to coveting. Why would the early commandments be so vague about actual human actions?

We are instructed to make no graven images of anything from land, sea, or sky. This commandment has been a cause of great division in Christianity. Catholics have argued that images of saints are permissible as they are a means of helping worshippers to focus on God. Protestants have argued such images are inherently idolatrous and encourage superstition. The destruction of these images by reforming Protestants was, of course, one of the features of the Reformation. They saw them as one of the key symbols of a decadent church.

The problem with the Ten Commandments is not just what they say but what they don't say. If they are a basic guide to morality, why do they set out rules about not desiring another man's wife and yet ignore prohibitions against truly important forms of harm? Where is the mention of serious crimes such as rape or the sexual abuse of a child? The reply you will often hear is that these are covered by the prohibition against adultery.

Let's examine why the claim that the commandment prohibiting adultery, covered other sexual acts, is a fiction. As we have already seen, the ancient Hebrew's attitude towards marriage differed radically from our modern one. The Ten Commandments did not prohibit polygamy; they did not prohibit a man from having concubines, in addition to his multiple wives and nor do they prohibit rape of very young women. This is not just an assumption; we have the evidence, and my source is the Bible's account of Moses after his forces had defeated the Midianites:

> And Moses was angry with the officers of the army, the commanders of thousands and the commanders of hundreds, who had come from service in the war. Moses said to them, 'Have you let all the women live? Behold, these, on Balaam's advice, caused the people of Israel to act treacherously against the Lord in the incident of Peor, and so the plague came among the congregation of the Lord. Now therefore, kill every male among the little ones, and kill every woman who has known man by lying with him. But all the young girls who have not known man by lying with him keep alive for yourselves.' (Num. 31: 14-18)

I think you'll have spotted that the commandment 'Thou shalt not kill' only applied to fellow Hebrews. It had no universal application. They intentionally killed defenceless men, women, and children. This is the man cited as the source for the commandment 'Thou shalt not Kill' indulging in genocide. And then he goes on to instruct his men to commit that other horrendous war crime, the rape of captured women. But not just women, he specifies very young women: virgins. Why virgins? The only explanation is so that his men would be the first to defile them. Let's be unequivocal about it; this is an account of Moses using rape as a weapon of war. We know about this; we know it has happened in modern times in conflict after conflict. We know it happened in the Second World War. We know it has happened in Colombia, Iraq, Afghanistan, Sudan, Chechnya, Nepal, Syria, and many other places. It is both done for sexual gratification and to send out a message. The message from Moses to anyone else who defied his army was: we will do worse than kill all of you, we will keep your young daughters alive and rape them. That is what the word 'terrorism' means. It is to use terror as a military weapon.

I have heard the most pathetic and cringing excuses for this. 'Oh, but they married some of them.' Where is the morality in claiming that the rape of a young girl is OK, if the victim is then forced to marry her attacker? Where would anyone get an idea as morally bankrupt as that from?

> If a man meets a virgin who is not betrothed, and seizes her and lies with her, and they are found, then the man who lay with her shall give to the father of the young woman fifty shekels of silver, and she shall be his

wife, because he has violated her. He may not divorce her all his days.
(Deut. 22: 28-29)

So you see a woman being forced to marry her rapist was built into the Law of Moses. The penalty on the man was financial and that he couldn't divorce her. She, on the other hand, had to spend her life with her rapist.

The morality of Moses was no different from the morality of Hitler, Pol Pot, and Stalin. It was the morality of the tyrant. Read the stories of biblical figures like Moses and Joshua, and you will see they are no more that deceitful, ruthless tyrants.

Chapter Twenty-One

Near-Death Experiences

I was very ill in the weeks before my sixth birthday. That was in the early months of 1968. My memory of that time is obviously vague, but what I do remember was a doctor shining a light in my mouth and the concern of my parents as he pronounced I had septicaemia. My parents were looking down at me, as I lay on the bed, but I was too drowsy to respond to their concern.

It must have been about 11 p.m. when a doctor was by my bed again. Whether I was able to read a clock or just heard it said, I don't recall. But I do recall the doctor by my bed. It was a cot in the sitting room. I assume that it was easier to keep a constant eye on me.

The doctor was very tall and thin, but I was looking down at where I lay. I was above and behind him and saw him lean over me to examine me. It was like I was sitting on a high shelf in a corner looking down. At the time it seemed a very natural place to be. I'd no idea what he was doing, but I recall him saying, 'It's all right. He's back.' His tone was apologetic, as though he had made a mistake.

Sometime later, after I eventually returned to school, I tried to tell a teacher about how I'd seen Jesus and how I'd met him. She said that, of course, I'd see Jesus when I died. But I was trying to tell her I'd already seen Jesus. She dismissed what I was saying, just as everybody else had. My parents hadn't wanted to know either. He'd looked like Jesus. He had long hair and had the type of dressing gown Jesus wore. I had known he was Jesus. I'd been walking along a dark road with the sun at the end of it, and I'd met him there.

For night after night, in my childhood, before I went to sleep, I remembered meeting Jesus. It was a reassuring image as I lay in bed each night.

How connected the 'out-of-body experience' and the meeting of Jesus were, I don't remember. The out-of-body experience seems to have formed my childhood idea of God and that was certainly connected with meeting Jesus in my young mind.

I am often contacted by those who claim that near-death experiences (NDEs) are evidence of an afterlife. The experience I have recounted above fits very much into what people class as a NDE. I don't, therefore, dispute that people have these experiences, but I am going to explain why these experiences do not provide evidence for either the existence of God or an afterlife.

Many years after the experience I have recounted, I was by now in my early forties, when I had the most painful experience of my life. My sister was stabbed to death by a former lover. I entered into the most unimaginable darkness and mental agony. In my grief, I looked for every spiritual answer. I began to explore NDEs, partly because my late sister had recounted her experience of one to me. That brought back my own experience. I read assiduously on the subject, not least the works of Raymond Moody.

Ray Moody, born in 1944 in the US state of Georgia, studied and eventually obtained a Ph.D. in Philosophy, before switching to medicine, had a major international success with his book Life After Life in 1975, a year before qualifying as an MD. He has dedicated his life to the subject of NDEs. He states that his interest in NDEs was first aroused by reading Plato. In his book The Republic, Plato recounts the story of Er, a soldier who woke up while lying on his funeral pyre and described how he had journeyed into the afterlife. Plato has been interpreted as integrating three elements of the NDE into his philosophy. These are: the departure of the soul from the cave of shadows (his metaphor for human ignorance) to see the light of truth, the flight of the soul to encounter a vision of a pure celestial being, and the recollection of the vision of light, which is what Plato sees as the purpose of philosophy. Moody began to address this experience in living people.

From a study of 150 people who had clinically died (their heart had stopped) or almost died, Moody concluded in Life After Life that there are nine experiences which are common amongst most people who have had a NDE. These are:

A buzzing or ringing noise
Peace and painlessness
Out-of-body experience
The tunnel experience
Rising rapidly into the Heavens
People of light
The being of light
The life review
Reluctance to return

Moody does not suggest that anyone must have had all these experiences, but that these are the common experiences. Nor did he claim this to be a scientific study. I certainly had an experience that was in accord with some items on this list. By the time I encountered the writings of Moody, I had left any Christianity long behind me but had spent years seeking spiritual understanding, from a variety of sources, and still saw Jesus as a spiritual archetype.

I was in a state of grief, and I was looking for clarity and comfort. Yet the more I read and thought about things, the more concerned I was with one big problem. If the afterlife is an objective experience, why it is always experienced through the religious and cultural experience of the person with the NDE? If Heaven was as Christians expect surely everyone would meet Jesus. However, Buddhists, Hindus, Muslims, and so on, all have NDE experiences in life with their own beliefs. The Jesus I had met was the Jesus most six-year-olds raised in a Christian culture would expect to meet. He was the one I had seen pictures of; the one I had been taught to expect.

Roughly speaking, before Constantine the Great, the images of Jesus in pictures and statues were beardless, boyish, and feminine, almost certainly modelled on Apollo. The more masculine-bearded image of Christ, which was modelled on Zeus, only came into vogue after the militaristic Constantine became a significant figure in Christianity and had used the cross as a lucky symbol in battle. This wasn't a precise shift but reflected a trend.

The idea of everyone meeting their own religious figure makes sense if those experiences arose from the imagination, but otherwise, it would suggest that every religion has its own version of the afterlife. You can't both argue that the afterlife is an objective experience and is as each person imagines it. That would mean all religions would have to be true. Even the grotesque vision of a man like Davis Koresh would have to be valid. This, and contradictions between religious beliefs, make this idea absurd.

Raymond Moody argues that people often make a decision to return to the world and that some don't decide to do so. But how can he know that there are those who decide not to? Since none, who have supposedly decided to remain, return he can't know that.

When I was about fifteen, a new game started in my all-boys school. We'd had rough games, and we'd been adventurous, but this game was the most dangerous of all. I was introduced to it by a boy we called Griff (an abbreviation of this surname, we didn't use first names). We weren't friends, but there was a respect between us. He was an able athlete and skilled on the football pitch. I was thin, awkward, and couldn't kick a ball straight if a fortune had depended on it. However, one day I'd challenged him to an arm wrestling match, and to his great surprise, as a result of weight training, I'd beaten him. It hadn't made us friends but had given him respect for me.

We were in a classroom without a teacher, and Griff told me he wanted to try an experiment, but he needed someone who was physically strong. I was sceptical, but he reassured me. I will not describe the technique as I have no wish to encourage it. It is sufficient to say it involved me holding my breath and an application of pressure to me. The result was my temporary unconsciousness.

I was going through a tunnel and then found myself lying in a boat, and a deep sea was all around me. In front of me was a sailing ship. Everything was so vivid. It was a warm summer's day, and above me was a perfect blue sky. I was bobbing up and down, feeling incredible content, without a care in the world.

I opened my eyes to find I was lying on the floor, and my classmates were gathered round me. I didn't want to be there. I wanted to be back on that boat. I'd glimpsed serenity, and I wanted it again.

What I had experienced was anoxia, the blocking of oxygen to the brain. Certainly not something fifteen-year-old boys should be encouraged to induce. A similar method, known as the fainting game, has led to a number of fatalities amongst teenagers.

What is notable was that I had an intensely vivid experience. This was a good deal stronger than normal sleeping dreams. The deprivation of oxygen led to the body collapsing, and yet the mind became more vivid. As Susan Blackmore explains:

> One might think anoxia cells would simply stop firing, but it does not work that way. There is now evidence that what actually happens is a shift in the balance between excitation and inhibition.

The most recent interview with Susan Blackmore, who is no longer researching this area, is a remarkable case of an interviewer seeking to blame someone for what others say of them. It reflects the lack of intellectual depth you often find from many who defend the idea that NDEs are evidence of an afterlife (see http://www.youtube. com/watch?v=SZ1nOiwHlLI).

On the other side of this debate, the reason why research from Susan Blackmore, which is now quite old, is turned to is quite simply because the claims in support of the idea of NDE are based on perceptions that seem hard to either support or refute, and there has, therefore, been a reluctance to tackle what seems to be such a pointless task.

It is the inhibitory connections that maintain the balance of the brain. Susan Blackmore goes on to explain that studies in rats show that in anoxia, inhibitory potentials are abolished before excitatory ones. To put it another way, the brain protects its capacity for consciousness above all other functions. This explains the vivid nature of my dream when put into consciousness. On later occasions, I had no recollection at all. There is no evidence of consistency in the brain's response. However, there does appear to be a possibility of either blankness or very vivid hallucinations. I doubt that there is an ethical way to fully explore this. I'd be very concerned if any scientific authority permitted the inducing of unconsciousness in this manner.

I was not dying, just playing a very foolish game; not only did I experience a powerful heavenly vision, but also I was very reluctant to return from it; a feature often noted in NDEs. It was the intensity of the experience that caused me to want to repeat the experiment on several further occasions, but I did not find that vision again.

We also know that the human brain can produce powerful hallucinatory experiences under the effects of psychedelic drugs or withdrawal of alcohol. Those who class NDEs as evidence of the afterlife need to explain why a powerful mental experience brought about by anoxia, or any other life-threatening experience, is any more reliable than those brought about by delirium tremors caused by alcohol withdrawal or the recreational use of drugs.

WHEN IS SOMEONE CONSCIOUS?

Most of us have had the experience of lying asleep, having a dream, hearing music or a voice in that dream, and waking up to find the music or voice was on a radio or someone speaking to us. So while we were asleep, we incorporated the sounds from the environment into our dream. Those who argue for an afterlife experience need to show that this does not happen in cases where they claim an out-of-body experience.

When someone is being resuscitated, medical staff are concerned about their heart and lung functions. They are not monitoring whether or not they are drifting from one level of consciousness to another. They may not be aware if a patient briefly opened their eyes. The patient may incorporate an image of the recovery room into their mental images and not be aware they had opened their eyes.

Dutch cardiologist, Pim Van Lommel MD, author of Consciousness Beyond Life, has claimed evidence that consciousness exists beyond the brain. He argues the people can recall NDEs that have happened when the brain was not functioning, when there was no neural activity. He relies very much on the research by Raymond Moody in defining these experiences.

However, what evidence is there that those experiences which are recalled later did not happen while the brain was going into and coming out of cardiac arrest? How can he show that deeply intense but short mental experiences don't appear to last a good deal longer than they are? Most of us only recall the dream we had shortly before awaking.

Van Lommel argues that people remember their lives and that memory is stored outside the brain. That is an extraordinary claim for which he has provided no evidence, whatsoever. It undermines any claim that he is reporting scientific evidence. For an interview with Pim van Lommel see http://www.e-ostadelahi.com/eoe-en/consciousness-and-near-death-experiences-pim-van-lommel/#video-lommel2

The onus of proof that NDEs are anything but a function of the brain is on those who claim it. They have not provided any evidence that withstands scrutiny.

QUESTIONS FOR THOSE WHO BELIEVE NDEs GIVE AN EXPERIENCE OF AN AFTERLIFE

- Why do you define death as a cardiac arrest rather than death of the brain?
- Why do you think NDEs have a fundamentally different mind-altering quality than the effects of alcohol withdrawal or use of psychedelic drugs?
- How does believing an experience, to be true, make it either real or unreal?

- How can you be certain when someone is fully unconscious, and just not apparently so but retaining a level of awareness?
- How can you be certain that the tunnel effect is not caused by the visual cortex?
- How can you deny that the deprival of air to brain (anoxia) can cause the effects identified in NDE and therefore show it is a physical response that does not require closeness to death?
- Why do people who are close to death because they are held at gunpoint and threatened not have NDEs?
- Why do those who have these experiences have them within the expectations of their religious and cultural experiences?

Chapter Twenty-Two

EVOLUTION

> Belief in evolution is a remarkable phenomenon. It is a belief passionately defended by the scientific establishment, despite the lack of any observable scientific evidence for macroevolution (that is, evolution from one distinct kind of organism into another). (Henry M. Morris, Ph.D., http://www.icr.org/home/resources/resources_tracts_scientificcaseagainstevolution/)

Well, that about raps it up for evolution. Send your Darwin books for recycling, and Dawkins will be only good for wood pulp. Anyway, it is time for a walk. There are some fine areas of woodland in this part of Northumberland. We saw a mole the other day. It ran straight across our path. In spring, we see goosanders on the river, the young chicks rushing behind their mother. In the autumn, we see salmon jumping. There is something we haven't seen for a while. Fifteen years ago, we knew which clump of trees to go to, and with patience, we'd see it. Ten years ago, it became a less common sight, and five years ago, we stopped seeing it at all. The creature I am talking about is the Eurasian red squirrel (Sciurus vulgaris). The British Isles have two species of squirrel: the red and the grey. You'll see the grey in many parks. They charge up and grab an abandoned sandwich, often only a few feet away from humans. The red is a much more timid creature. You are more likely to see it scampering up a tree, and when we did, it would fill our hearts with joy, such a beautiful little creature. How we miss it.

The reason for the decline of the red squirrel is easily summed up: the grey squirrel (Sciurus carolinensis).

Red Squirrels North England (RSNE) explains the situation as follows:

> The Red Squirrel (Sciurus vulgaris) is a priority species for conservation in the UK. Its dramatic decline in the UK the last century has been attributed to the introduction and spread of the North American Grey Squirrel (Sciurus carolinensis), both through direct competition for resources as well as disease-mediated competition with the grey squirrel acting as a reservoir for the Squirrelpox virus (SQPV). (http://www.rsne. org.uk/sites/default/files/RSNE%20Project%20Summary_0.pdf)

So it is not that the grey squirrels are bashing the reds over the head and killing them. It is that the grey are better adapted to the environment and better at finding food (in this case, they can more easily digest acorns). No one has made a decision that the greys will survive better than the reds. In fact, the only intentional intervention has been to protect the reds from the powerful effect of competition from the greys.

Hold on, I've read about this somewhere. I'm sure I have read about how one species dies out because it can't survive in a changed environment and another thrives because it can. I'll just check my bookshelves. Not there. Let me just look in the recycling pile.

> Dominant species belonging to the larger group tend to give birth to new and dominant forms so that each large group tends to become still larger, and at the same time more divergent in character. But as all groups cannot thus succeed in increasing in size, for the world would not hold them, the most dominant groups beat the less dominant. (Chapter XIV, On the Origin of Species, Charles Darwin)

So the reds are pushed out because the greys are better at finding food, and of course, if you believe in Creationism, how can you escape the conclusion that God knowingly created both species of squirrel knowing how the grey would push the red out of its environment.

For those who are not Creationists, I should point out that these highly imaginative ideas come in two forms of packaging: 'Creationism' and 'Intelligent Design'. Both see life as having been created by an intelligent being.

They argue that obviously humans are able to develop new plants or breeds of dog, but that is seen as working with creation. All the materials of creation, and forms of life, were originally put on Earth by an intelligent being and put there in basically the form we find them in today. They do accept the idea of microevolution. This is accounted for by what Conservapedia tells us is:

> Broadly defined, as the inevitable small-scale changes in allele frequencies in a population within the same species.

Alleles are genes that account for variations in phenotypic character (height, hair colour, etc.). Where their understanding of this process differs from the mainstream, scientific understanding is that they argue that microevolution remains within a species and never leads to a new species. They see it as a variation that is built into the design of a species.

This they usually believe happened in the past 10,000 years, and there has been no evolutionary development from one species to another. This is believed by many evangelical churches, Conservative Muslims, and some Orthodox Jews.

WHAT IS THE DIFFERENCE BETWEEN CREATIONISM AND INTELLIGENT DESIGN?

Creationists believe in the Bible creation story as literally true. God made the world in seven days (six since he rested on the Sabbath). Adam and Eve were the first humans. They see the explanation of how the world came about as essentially a matter of faith. Well, at least this version has a talking snake and the idea that the first woman emerged from the rib of a man in a deep sleep or coma. That is a decent mythology.

However, if you accept the biblical story of creation, you need to explain why you prefer that to any other mythological tale. Why accept the claims of the powerful God of the Abrahamic tradition rather than Zulu mythology, where Unkulunkulu emerges from the reeds and is the first man, or Vishvakarman in Vedic mythology, who created the Earth and Heavens? Don't most of those who accept the biblical account do so because it is the story they were told in childhood and know best? Why should the version of the story you know best be the true one?

What these versions have in common is the idea that some form of powerful being caused the world to come into existence. This was also at a time when gods were used to explain the weather, and spirits explained disease.

This idea of a divine being who intentionally created the universe is one of the most common arguments for the existence of God. Yet there is no coherent explanation for why such a being is necessary. One typical line of argument (argument may be too grand a term here) will run that there is evidence of a creator all around us. Birds sing to the glory of God. The belief is that God made birds to add beauty to his creation and that could not have been accidental. Their song is a testimony to the wonder of God. Birds, therefore, could not exist without the intention of a creator. This is an attitude that is found in both Creationist and non-Creationist believers. The non-Creationists will simply interpose evolution as God's method for allowing the development of birds as a species, whereas Creationists will see sparrows and robins as having been directly created by God.

The problem with this argument is that those who see a creator as the purpose for the beginning of the universe often mistake cause and intention. That there needs to be a cause for any event is very different from saying that there needs to be someone who intended it to happen. The world is filled with examples of things that happen which no one intended to happen. The most common argument of believers is that the universe had to come from somewhere; after all, nothing comes from nothing. The first logical difficulty with this is they then contradict their own assertion by arguing for a God who has no origin, who is simply the unexplained origin of all things. None of them has yet come up with a coherent explanation of why it makes more sense to say God, for whom there is no evidence, had no creator than to say the universe had no creator. After all, we can, at least, demonstrate that the universe exists.

There is no evidence of a divine being needed to set off aspects of nature; there is no evidence of God setting off the spring or winding the slowing down natural processes in autumn (or the fall, as some will call it). Why was there any need for him to have started the whole natural process in the first place? It is true that humans can manage and alter aspects of nature, but the point is nature is very capable of getting along without that type of intervention. Great rivers and forests have developed without anyone taking any action to bring them about. There is nothing in the natural world that shows that it needs divine intervention. So how does the 'Someone must have done it' argument apply? How is it any more valid than the belief that God directly makes the rain?

The one thing believers will still argue is that as nothing comes from nothing, the godless view of the universe makes no sense. I am often told 'You just believe that the universe popped up out of nowhere.' The truth is that religion does not even have the most poetic explanation for how this world came about.

> The amazing thing is that every atom in your body came from a star that exploded. And, the atoms in your left hand probably came from a different star than your right hand. It really is the most poetic thing I know about physics: You are all stardust. You couldn't be here if stars hadn't exploded, because the elements—the carbon, nitrogen, oxygen, iron, all the things that matter for evolution—weren't created at the beginning of time. They were created in the nuclear furnaces of stars, and the only way they could get into your body is if those stars were kind enough to explode. So, forget Jesus. The stars died so that you could be here today. (Lawrence M. Krauss, A Universe from Nothing: Why There Is Something Rather Than Nothing)

The denial of evolution is often masked as a call for freedom of belief. But the facts about how the world has come into being and been developed are not a question of belief. The evidence tells us that we are the outcome of a very, very long process.

Now if we deny that, we don't just deny evolution, we deny just about everything we know about chemistry and physics and, it goes without saying, we throw out a fundamental plank of biology, and by and by we'd need to deny everything we know about geology (as mountains were made over millions of years), and we'd have to completely ignore anything but the most rudimentary knowledge of astronomy, and let's be honest there wouldn't be much left of our knowledge of science. The denial of evolution is an attack on the human intellect; it is a fundamental denial of the advance of human understanding. What complicates this argument for an intention is that believers give the being they attribute responsibility for it a personality.

The God they imagine to have intentionally created the world is usually imagined as some form of superhuman or other creature. In Theism, they will even call him names like Father. So their argument is not just that there is a creator but that he is a benevolent one. The creation of the world was a benevolent act by a loving God, and they see maintaining the belief that he created all of existence as a sign of loyalty to him. They have an emotional investment in the idea of a creator God.

It is not difficult to understand why early societies worshipped a creator God. It provided them with a means to seek control over the power of the weather and of managing many other unpredictable aspects of their life such as the success of the hunt or abundance of their crops. If there was a supernatural being who was responsible for everything, there was someone to appeal to who could mitigate the effects of an uncertain world.

This idea remains essentially at the heart of modern Theism. Modern believers may not pray about the weather, but for them, faith in God is still to a large degree about seeking to find control in an uncertain world. It is often said that it is fear of what happens after death that keeps people loyal to religion, but the fear of having no force to appeal to over life's trials and unexpected turns is just as important. It may, in many cases, be a great deal more so. In essence, many people believe that God must have made the world because they desperately want someone to be in control. The problem is that wanting something is not evidence that the desired thing exists.

In contrast, Darwin started with the evidence. Because Darwin neglected to provide a bibliography at the end of his most famous work On the Origin of Species, there are those who will argue that he was not a real scientist. The impression is given that he sat around and thought up a few ideas which he managed to convince others of.

He spent years, most notably on the voyage of the Beagle between 1831 and 1836, but also years back in England when he researched into subjects as varied as pigeon breeding and The Formation of Vegetable Mould through the Action of Worms, with Observations on Their Habits, which was published at the end of his life. One of the reasons he took so long between the first drafts of On the Origin of Species and the final publication, which was prompted by Alfred Russell Wallace independently arriving at the same conclusion, was that Darwin felt his theory had to be thoroughly tested. He had to be sure it would withstand scientific scrutiny. He had to be certain that he had the evidence.

One important example was the observations he had meticulously made on his visits to the Galápagos Islands in 1835. He noted the varieties of finch and collected specimens for later study. He stated that:

> Seeing this gradation and diversity of structure in one small, intimately related group of birds, one might really fancy that from an original paucity of birds in this archipelago, one species had been taken and modified for different ends. (Voyage of the Beagle, 1844)

At this point, he was making a tentative suggestion, but he was making it on the basis of strong evidence. Even this was less tentative than an earlier version, this was not someone who was rushing to a conclusion. We see how he is more certain in his use of the evidence later.

> The naturalist, looking at the inhabitants of these volcanic islands in the Pacific, distant several hundred miles from the continent, yet feels that he is standing on American land. Why should this be so? why should the species which are supposed to have been created in the Galapagos Archipelago, and nowhere else, bear so plain a stamp of affinity to those created in America? There is nothing in the conditions of life, in the geological nature of the islands, in their height or climate, or in the proportions in which the several classes are associated together, which resembles closely the conditions of the South American coast: in fact there is a considerable dissimilarity in all these respects. On the other hand, there is a considerable degree of resemblance in the volcanic nature of the soil, in climate, height, and size of the islands, between the Galapagos and Cape de Verde Archipelagos: but what an entire and absolute difference in their inhabitants! The inhabitants of the Cape de Verde Islands are related to those of Africa, like those of the Galapagos to America. I believe this grand fact can receive no sort of explanation on the ordinary view of independent creation; whereas on the view here maintained, it is obvious that the Galapagos Islands would be likely to receive colonists, whether by occasional means of transport or by formerly continuous land, from America; and the Cape de Verde Islands from Africa; and that such colonists would be liable to modification;—the principle of inheritance still betraying their original birthplace. (On the Origin of Species, 1859)

141

What Darwin is saying is that the variations in these birds, which were found to differ from island to island, can be explained by how each species having developed separately rather than by an intentional design. Darwin didn't invent an idea out of thin air. He had the evidence before him. He was able to measure and accurately record the differences in these birds. It is because his conclusions were based on sound evidence that they are held to be true by almost all scientists today. There are, of course, a small number of exceptions. These scientists are largely those outside this area and a number motivated by religion. What alternative do they present? They have nothing, but dull idea of a world made by creator.

Humans in culture after culture created myths of beings who created the world. They created the idea that there was a force that was stronger than the elements. However, unless ground is barren, vegetation grows without human intervention. When a forest grows up, there is no need for humans to sculpt the trees. Humans may wish to manage the woodland, but it can grow up very well without human help. Humans may be busy depleting the stock of fish in the sea, but they didn't need to put them there in the first place. In each of these cases, human intervention is as likely, and often more likely, to do harm than good. In all, there is no evidence of a divine being at work. What people cling to, today, is the idea that there is a being who can decide events in their favour. In order to do that, they need to believe in a world that was intentionally created.

The idea of Intelligent Design is most vigorously defended by the Discovery Institute, which argues the case made in 1802 by William Paley. Paley argued that if you found a watch and examined it, you could only conclude that it had been intentionally made and skilfully designed. The same principles must apply to the creation of the world. Those supporting Intelligent Design argue that there is scientific evidence which shows that the universe must have been created by an intelligent being.

This differs from the approach of theistic evolution or evolutionary creation. It accepts the evolutionary process but sees it as a tool of God's creation. This is accepted by the Catholic Church and most mainstream Protestant churches.

The third approach rejects any divine role in evolution and sees evolution as having shaped the nature of all life without the intervention of a divine being at any stage. This, of course, is the position most Atheists hold. Just let me fetch a book from the wood pulp pile:

Richard Dawkins's The Blind Watchmaker (1986)

> Paley's argument is made with passionate sincerity and is informed
> by the best biological scholarship of the day, but it is wrong, gloriously
> and utterly wrong. The analogy between telescope and eye, between
> watch and living organism, is false. All appearances to the contrary, the

only watchmaker in nature is the blind force of physics, albeit deployed in a special way. A true watchmaker has foresight: he designs his cogs and springs, and plans their interconnections, with a future purpose in his mind's eye. Natural selection, the blind unconscious, automatic process which Darwin discovered, and which we now know is the explanation for the existence and apparently purposeful form of all life has no purpose in mind. It has no mind and no mind's eye. It does not plan for the future. It has no vision, no foresight, no sight at all. If it can be said to play the role of watchmaker in nature, it is the blind watchmaker.

TERMINOLOGY AND ITS MISUSE

A great deal of the argument over evolution has surrounded terminology. The phrase 'Theory of Evolution' is often misunderstood. It is often said that it is 'only a theory'. The first point is to address the word 'theory'. People use the word in the meaning of 'Well, the theory is that there is a bus every fifteen minutes, but I've tested it, and it doesn't work.' That is not what is meant in scientific terms.

> The word 'theory' can be used to mean something speculative and tentative. In everyday speech it probably usually is used in that sense. Scientists very often use it in a much more positive sense. I think the easiest way is to use the ordinary language word 'fact'. In the ordinary language sense of the word fact, evolution is a fact. (Richard Dawkins, 'The Fact of Evolution', Bigthink.com, 26 October 2009)

A scientific theory is 'a well-substantiated explanation of some aspect of the natural world, based on a body of facts that have been repeatedly confirmed through observation and experiment.' (National Academy of Sciences (1999), http://www.nap.edu)

This description applies fairly to evolution, which has had its claims checked in many ways, and from Darwin's time on, experimentation has been used to look at questions such as how species have adapted. So let us be very clear a theory in science is not just an idea. So to apply that meaning of theory to the regularity of buses we need to be able to say, 'I've meticulously researched the records for the past century, and the evidence shows that a bus regularly failed to arrive at fifteen intervals throughout all that time, and then had another two experts in the "bus timetable checking field", double-check, and closely examine my findings. Even then you'd need to check for other factors, such as how the changes in timetables related to actual arrival times of buses and may have affected the result. This would still go nowhere near the evidence provided for evolution, but it shows that a theory is about serious evidence.'

The 'survival of the fittest' is another misconstrued term and is often thought to mean the survival of the strongest and most ruthless. It was not in fact a term originally used by Charles Darwin in On the Origin of Species but was first used by Herbert Spencer in his Principles of Biology (1864), five years after Darwin's great work was published. This wrong interpretation has been used to, in some cases, justify the most unpleasant of ideas such as fascism and eugenics. They both used distortions of Darwin's ideas to justify cruelly mistreating people. Nazism used it to claim racial superiority, and those supporting eugenics used it as an excuse to forcibly sterilise young women whom they regarded as intellectually deficient. Laws were passed in over thirty states in the USA allowing for the compulsory sterilisation of those considered 'mentally unfit'. This was often combined with racism and a desire to punish prostitutes.

This terrible history has often been used to seek to discredit Darwin's claims. An important point needs to be made. The hatred of those who used Darwin to justify those terrible acts was based on their beliefs, rather than on the evidence for evolution. The Theory of Evolution is simply the use of the available evidence to establish what is true about the history of how life on Earth has developed. The misuse of what is true does not make it untrue. Because tsunamis cause terrible destruction does not make them fictional. The grotesque and ugly twisting of Darwin's understanding does not make it untrue. However, there continues to be those who will try to argue that evolution constitutes an immoral idea.

One terrible example of this was when following the murder of twelve young people and children, and the injury of thirty-eight more, in a midnight cinema showing of the new Batman film, in Aurora near Denver, Colorado, on 20 July 2012, evangelical pastor Rick Warren tweeted:

> When students are taught they are no different from animals, they act like it.

He later retracted this tweet, but it does reflect a very confused way of thinking. A scientific theory is rejected because it is seen as immoral. This is oddly applied to evolution and not to any explanation of diseases. Surely, if the natural world was intrinsically moral, there would be evidence of it being consistently so. But where is this evidence of an intrinsic morality in 'God's creation'?

The logic of Rick Warren's argument is that God created the lion to tear the deer to pieces and did so deliberately and intentionally. That would have to be intrinsically moral. Surely, intentional cruelty carries a moral failing which unintentional cruelty never can. A God who deliberately designed such cruelty would have to be an intentionally cruel God. The God who designed human nature knowing it would lead to mass murder can't escape responsibility for doing so. However, Rick Warren seems to want one law of morality for God and another for humans. He seems to think it is OK for God to knowingly create a cruel situation, but not for humans to do so. He can't then argue that the love humanity should aspire to is God's love.

Another objection is to the term 'survival of the fittest'. This is often seen as supporting the idea that the bullies of nature get all the spoils. The word 'fittest' is often misunderstood to mean strongest. What it means is the survival of those best adapted to the environment. If this only meant the strongest, only the largest and most powerful species would have survived. Yet in fact, it is the smallest of living forms that are most populous on the planet. Being very small is no barrier to the existence of bacteria or insects.

What 'survival of the fittest' means is that only the species of plants or animals that get the necessary food, water, and sufficient protection from harmful elements to survive long enough to reproduce get their genes passed on. So every living thing that exists has ancestors who have done that. None of us would be here if our ancestors had not had these things for long enough to reproduce.

So How Does That Lead to Selection?

First, it already excludes anyone who dies too young to reproduce. The second thing it does is favour the traits most useful for survival. So let us say a creature lives in a forest where there are predators that can't climb trees, roaming the ground. Those hunted creatures which can climb trees will survive. Their brothers and sisters who can't climb would have much less chance of survival. So the next generation would be descended from good climbers. This is where genetics come in. If the factor that allows for effective tree climbing is long legs, the only way that physical characteristic can be passed on to the next generation is through genes. This will be a gradual process. So within a litter, there will be shorter—and longer-legged young. Over many generations of the longer-legged ones surviving, that will become the dominant character.

It is important to note that there is no intentional process in this. Leg length naturally varies. Those with longer legs only survive because they can climb trees, and they go on to survive through the generations and become characteristic of the species only because they are the ones to survive. So when we say selection, we don't mean a choice like deciding between options in a box of chocolates.

Characteristics develop out of necessity and often remain when they are redundant. A characteristic which will not prevent reproduction will remain, even when it may be harmful, while one which prevents reproduction will not be passed on simply because it can't be. The survivors become the future of the species. As Richard Dawkins puts it in Climbing Mount Improbable:

> It just is the case that some offspring are more likely to die while others have what it takes to survive and reproduce. Therefore as the generations go by, the average, typical, creature in the population becomes even better at the art of surviving and reproducing.

When explaining the role of genes, Richard Dawkins goes on to say:

> In the wake of a greatly enlarged nose, since the trunk increases the weight of the head, the bones of the neck will need to be strengthened. The balance of the whole body may change, with further knock-on effects, perhaps on the backbone and the pelvis.

Natural selection is simply understood as necessary change for survival. Consider that the fate of around 99 per cent of all species has been to go extinct. The American Museum of Natural History regards this as an underestimate. There is no evidence of any intentional force, other than human effort, to prevent the extinction of species. The only reason any species survives is because it is able to. It gets the necessities for life. The origins of that evolutionary process go back a long way.

Richard Dawkins's great contribution has been on the role of genetics. He has explored the relationship between genetic variations which arise by chance, due to the genetic code being copied inaccurately and the role of natural selection which allows the variations which allow for the individuals to survive long enough to reproduce to pass these on. This brings about changes over a very long period of time.

In The Magic of Reality, Richard Dawkins calculates that you would need to go back through 185-million generations to find the first evidence of a life form which humanity has evolved from. The important point is that nothing in the evidence for those generations all the way back to your 185-millionth-great-grandfather, as Dawkins puts it, contradicts the evidence for evolution. Let's be clear Creationists and Intelligent Design advocates have made many claims, but they have found nothing that can be objectively shown to contradict the evidence for evolution. They do make attempts to question the biological evidence. They claim there are gaps in the fossil record.

> If evolution happened, the fossil record should show continuous and gradual changes from the bottom to the top layers. Actually, many gaps or discontinuities appear throughout the fossil record. (Center for Scientific Creation, http://www.creationscience.com/onlinebook/LifeSciences27.html)

The above quotation is very typical of the approach and argument found among those who argue against evolution. The first point to make is that many organisms don't fossilise well, and in fact, fossils only survive in good environmental conditions. These conditions are not that common. Fossilisation does not happen automatically to bones. Something has to happen to cause fossilisation. As David Kopaska-Merkel, Staff Hydrogeology Division, Geological Survey of Alabama, explains:

We can look at fossilization processes operating today, and see the effects in very young fossils (thousands of years old). For example, organic material in hot springs can become completely encased in calcium carbonate crystals in only hours. Therefore, any fossil that is millions of years old has had time, at least, to become fully mineralized. (http://www. madsci.org/posts/archives/1999-11/943381960.Ch.r.html)

Here, we have an example of a chemical reaction that causes fossilisation. We can also think of how mummification preserved Egyptian corpses. They only survived because the body was protected. To therefore argue that there should not be gaps in the fossil record shows a lack of understanding of the process of fossilisation.

The story of evolution is the history of every living thing we know. It is truly a wonder. You can, of course, opt for a dull myth that contradicts itself, explains nothing, and sees humanity as the plaything of a celestial tyrant. I'd recommend the more interesting option.

Chapter Twenty-Three

THE GOD OF DISASTERS

When there is a major natural disaster, there is always a big call to pray for the survivors. To believe in a God who can help in any way, you need to believe in a God who can intervene in the world, and who can decide when to do so and when not to do so; if not, there would be no point in prayer. You also need to believe in a God with sufficient knowledge of the world to see where the problems lie.

This raises a very simple question: if a God can intervene after a disaster, why was he unable or unwilling to intervene before it happened?

We seem to be faced with the possibility of a God who claims to be all loving, all powerful, and all knowing and yet does nothing to prevent suffering and afterwards expects people to beg for help. We are all familiar with the argument that disasters bring people to faith, but we never get an explanation of why an all-powerful being needs to resort to such tactics.

It is often said that disasters are sent to test us. Why would an all-knowing God need to test people, when he'd know the outcome beforehand? He'd not need to find out who was worthy as he'd know already. The need to allow people to act on 'free will' makes no sense for natural disasters or children and other innocent victims in disasters.

The very act of pleading to a God for help implies he needs to be prompted to compassion. Why would an all-loving being need to be reminded of his duty to help the suffering?

Prayer after a disaster is the response of 'Someone must be able to do something.' However, wanting there to be an all-powerful being that can intervene does not mean that being exists. It is said that the belief brings people comfort. But does it? My recollection of prayers of desperation is not of comfort but of a refusal to accept situations I could not change. That sometimes removed my focus from what I could do in practical terms.

There is the claim that such prayers give people strength. Do they? Where is the evidence that the fire fighter who prays is any more effective than the one who doesn't? Where is the verifiable evidence that praying after a disaster has any meaningful effect? Is it not just a one-way process?

A DOG'S BELIEF

Chapter Twenty-Four

THOU SHALT HAVE NO FALSE DOGS BEFORE ME

Near where I live, there is a stone statue of a large dog. It sits in a garden, high above the road on which I used to walk my dog, Becky. When we'd pass it, she'd get very excited. She'd bark at it and want to run at it. She seemed to be convinced that it was a real dog and that it was ready to charge at her. She needed to warn it off. You might think that because it didn't react, she'd soon realise it was inanimate. But no. In fact, as we'd approach that house, Becky seemed to prepare herself to face the large dog that stared imperiously down at her. What appeared to be happening is that the memory of her previous reactions had strengthened her conviction. She interpreted the statue to be a real dog and was very certain in her interpretation. That this 'dog' had never barked at her didn't run at her or wag its tail, and that it had no dog smell or any other sign of life did not deter her belief that it was a living being. It was her belief, not the reality that she acted upon.

Of course, religious faith is more complex than a reaction to a stone dog, but the same process is going on. Faith is built up through the believer's own reactions to religious ideas. They often build a relationship with God in their own mind. They interpret the world in the light of this idea. They attribute events in their life, and even some of the feelings they have, to this idea. They create expectations based on their ideas. They develop the idea of God as a living being.

All they need, for this process, is the belief there is a God. They do not need any verifiable evidence that God actually exists, and yet they can be very resistant to suggestion he doesn't. Just as the statue seems to give confirmation and reinforcement of Becky's belief, so it is that going to church, the Bible and prayer, confirm and reinforce the faith of the believer. Since we can reasonably assume that the human imagination is more sophisticated than that of a dog, it is not difficult to account for the more sophisticated idea of God. However, the essence of the two experiences seems to be very similar.

There is no evidence that a prayerful relationship with God is anything more than a one-way process and that believers find confirmation in anything more than their store of previous reactions to prayer. There is nothing to show that what believers perceive as the presence of God is any more real than Becky's imagined presence of a dog.

When believers talk about a relationship with God, there is no evidence of anything but their projection of a relationship on to a being they imagine to be responding to them. Yet somehow they often have a relationship which ignores the dark side, like a God who created a world where most people will end up in Hell.

From the cruelty and stupidity of belief in Demons, Heaven and Destiny to freedom.

Chapter Twenty-Five

DEMONS

If you have ever watched Buffy the Vampire Slayer, the spin-off Angel, or any of the many other vampire-related dramas, you will be familiar with the concept of demons. They range from the mindlessly violent to the comical. Some even manage to combine these concepts. Most of us will be willing to suspend a little disbelief, as we watch such entertainment. When it ends, we return to our world where we have no belief in such beings. Yet not everyone does. One of the most cruel, sinister, and harmful aspects of religion arises from those who actually believe demons exist, and worse than that, they believe that they possess children.

> Namita, 18, had suffered under the bondage of demon possession for several months. Family members took the young woman to many shrines, sorcerers and psychological specialists. Although they spent nearly 15,000 rupees (approximately US$300), seeking a cure for her, their efforts were in vain. Namita's parents and her extended family worried about her future.
>
> Then their neighbors told them about Puneet, a national missionary who lived nearby. At the family's request Puneet visited their house and prayed for Namita's deliverance. The believers in Puneet's church also joined in prayer.
>
> Within a few days, Namita was completely free. Puneet explained the Gospel to Namita's family, telling them of the need for salvation. After listening carefully, Namita and her family decided to follow Jesus.
>
> Today Namita is vocal about her faith, and she also desires to serve the Lord in her village.

This article appeared in the January 2013 edition of SEND! (Gospel for Asia news magazine). The publication is filled with accounts of miraculous healings, cures, and liberation from demonic forces. It declares 'Nothing is impossible for God, who has defeated Satan.'

The magazine is published and distributed by Gospel for Asia, a large international missionary organisation with administrative offices in the United States, Australia, New Zealand, South Africa, and the United Kingdom. The organisation was founded and is run by K. P. Yohannan, a Pentecostal pastor, who was controversially consecrated as an Anglican Archbishop in the Church of South India. The headquarters are in Carrollton, Fort Worth, Texas.

In parts of the world where the idea of demons is still strong, as this article shows, Christians, backed with money and support from large developed countries, use the fear of demons to spread Christianity. They exploit fears of dark forces for their own ends.

We don't know what was happening to Namita. She may have being going through a psychological or psychiatric difficulty, or simply, like eighteen-year-olds all over the world, wanted to behave in ways that her family disapproved of. What we can say is that there has never been any evidence produced to support claims of demonic possession. We can also say that K. P. Yohannan has built up a large international and wealthy organisation (about which a number of questions are now being asked by tax authorities) on this type of claim.

This is a Christian organisation with Western money that is willing to exploit beliefs that would not be taken seriously in any industrialised country, in order to promote Christianity. Why should we take the claims of demonic possession in the New Testament any more seriously?

Yet this issue is alive in Pentecostal churches in Western countries today. In 'Branded a Witch', which is one of the most moving documentaries I have ever watched, Kevani Kanda tracked how young British children were sent to the Congo to have what was variously termed witchcraft, or demonic possession, treated. There was the distressing case of a five-year-old boy being imprisoned in a church and deprived of food and all but a minimal amount of water for three days because he was deemed to be a demon. Kevani Kanda, whose biography is in preparation, had experienced the abuse of being branded in this way as a child.

Pentecostalism is a very major part of Christianity. It has to accept that it is perpetuating beliefs that are causing serious harm. This is serious child abuse. Pentecostal preachers in Britain and the United States who preach about demons need to understand that they are providing justification for terrible child abuse in places like the Congo.

Chapter Twenty-Six

HEAVEN

Who will get into Heaven? Religion is often assumed to make a promise of eternal life. That must be the one of the vaguest and most self-contradictory promises in history. The one thing we can say about entry into Heaven is that there is no agreement amongst Christians as to who will get in.

One claim is that only those who are raptured by Christ will get into Heaven. This could be a very exclusive category as it is argued there are only 144,000 places.

> And I looked, and, lo, a Lamb stood on the mount Sion, and with him
> an hundred forty and four thousand, having his Father's name written in
> their foreheads. (Rev. 14: 1)

As this includes all those who are 'Dead in Christ', anyone hoping for entry not only needs to compete against all living Christians but against all who have lived in the past 2,000 years. It is not difficult to reach a probability of a million to one chance of getting into Heaven. Even very few of the estimated 800-900 million evangelical Christians in the world (estimate according to the Center for the Study of Global Christianity 2011) would stand any chance of getting into Heaven. That is the measure of the extraordinary level of egotism it takes to believe you'd get into Heaven under such conditions. You have to wonder why a God would create a world where so very few would get into Heaven. After all, the mathematics of it all would not be news to him.

An alternative view is that anyone who has turned their life over to Christ (been saved) will get into Heaven. This excludes many other Christians (who have not been saved), those of all other religions and, of course, those who are non-believers. I have heard Christians defending this, and their position is to in effect to blame anyone who is not saved for rejecting Christ. The logic of that position is a child with Hindu or Muslim parents, who dies of hunger, should have somehow realised Christ was the redeemer and rejected their faith. That would not have saved them from starvation but would have got them into Heaven.

A more liberal view is that anyone who has led a good life will get into Heaven. Here there is a difference of opinion, with other Christians, over whether or not those who will get into Heaven need to have accepted Christ.

Islam is no more certain over who will find eternal life. Despite the claim being widely advertised, there is no reference to a reward of 72 virgins in the Qur'an; however, what it does say still raises some very serious questions. The 72 virgins reference is found in Jami` at-Tirmidhi, a text revered to by Sunni Muslims, but there are arguments this might have been mistranslated and it may have been 72 angels.

The relevant text in the Qur'an is Surah 78: 31-34.

The Abdullah Yusuf Ali translation, the most frequently used version of the Qur'an in English, has it as:

> Lo! for the duteous is achievement—Gardens enclosed and vineyards, And maidens for companions, And a full cup.

The A.J. Arberry translation has it as:

> Surely for the god fearing awaits a place of security, gardens and vineyards and maidens with swelling breasts, like of age, and a cup overflowing.

What is apparent is that a number of translators left out the reference to women's breasts out of embarrassment. The reference is in the earliest known versions of the text. Even if we accept that supposed incentive to suicide bombers, the 72 virgins fantasy, is an idea that seems to border on paedophilia and implies that men want women that are barely more than girls rather than more mature women. While this is not in the Qur'an, we are still faced with a major problem over this Islam's attitude towards women. You will note that it does not differ from the attitude attributed to Moses, earlier.

Whatever way you read this text, the idea that women are being given as a reward is unavoidable. The reference to swelling breasts, more overtly, suggests their sexuality, but even if it was not there, we still have women, very young women, as a commodity that is given to men. There is no suggestion that these women could either give or withdraw their consent to this situation. Any argument that the Qur'an respects women and protects them is contradicted by these verses. A woman who is given as a reward is being treated as no more than a slave.

As for what life is like in Heaven, we are given little information. Frankly, it all sounds pretty boring. All that harp music could get tedious, and there'd be no sneaking bars of chocolate or other misbehaving. It really seems like it would be sedate and devoid of fun. Why would anyone want an eternity like that?

Chapter Twenty-Seven

THERE IS NO SUCH THING AS A COINCIDENCE

One way of thinking which is common to many, but not all believers, is to find meaning and connections where none exist. Many believers use phrases such as 'There is no such thing as a coincidence', 'Everything happens for a reason', 'These things are meant to be', or that old favourite 'God has a plan for every one of us'. They look for evidence of a divine hand in everything. They are convinced that the will of God is constantly at work in the world. We could call this 'guiding hand' thinking.

The claim is that when events occur that are outside what you'd expect according to the laws of probability, they are somehow special. Instead of understanding that probability means that events of low probability will sometimes happen, many believers use the apparent improbability of an event as evidence that a miraculous force is at work. They assume that if something that appears to be unlikely happens, it must have been the result of an intentional cause. They dismiss any possibility of simple chance and hail the smallest of events as the wonder of God working in their lives.

But unlikely coincidences do happen. If you buy a ticket in the main draw of the UK lottery, your chances of winning are approximately fourteen million to one. But people do win the lottery, and for each of them, that is an improbable outcome. But consider how much more improbable it would be if no one ever won the lottery. That would be deeply suspicious and almost certainly fraudulent.

But believers will try to claim the lottery is an exception. They will usually refer to personal incidents in their lives which are signs of a divine intervention. They will point to a coalition of events which has confirmed their faith and demonstrate the power of God or Jesus in their life or whatever source they attribute their fortune to.

But the most unlikely coincidences do happen even to Atheists, and I have a personal experience which shows that they do. In fact, I need go no further that the room I am sitting in as I write this. I'm in the study in my house. The house was built about 160 years ago (about 58,440 days). I just thought I'd let you know that figure because it will be useful later. These walls have been papered and painted numerous times. It was impossible to say what I'd find as I peeled off the paper. I wondered if I'd find Victorian wallpaper.

You must understand that my motives were pure. I wasn't simply doing this to find any excuse not to sit in front of a computer and write. This was a need for a creative distraction. I expected days of laboriously scraping paper from the wall. I started by pulling at paper that was detached just above the skirting board. To my surprise, all the layers of paper had formed a stiff card and came away easily. It was when I turned the paper over that I made my discovery. The last layer of paper was newspaper. Why it was used I could not say, but I looked to see when the newspaper was from and the date was very readable. Checking the sheets, I saw the same day's paper had been used again and again. That date on the paper was 14 June 1954. That date began to whizz around in my head. I was sure it was in some way significant. At first, I recalled that one of my school friends had that birthday, though not that year (neither he nor I are quite that old). Anyway, a birthday is only a 365.25 to one probability and hardly significant.

I did the only reasonable thing anyone can do with such curiosity. I googled the date. The first thing that came up was the Pledge of Allegiance to the US Flag. It was the last change in the Pledge of Allegiance and occurred on 14 June (Flag Day) 1954 when President Dwight D. Eisenhower approved adding the words 'under God'. As he authorised this change, Eisenhower stated:

> In this way we are reaffirming the transcendence of religious faith in America's heritage and future; in this way we shall constantly strengthen those spiritual weapons which forever will be our country's most powerful resource, in peace or in war. http://en.wikipedia.org/wiki/Pledge_of_ Allegiance—cite_note-14("'God iIn America: God in the White House'". PBS.)

Eisenhower was effectively declaring war on Atheism, a battle still carried on by the Christian right today.

I am writing a book about freedom from religion, and I found a newspaper on my wall dated from a day of deep significance to this issue. Nothing more clearly exemplifies the imposition of religion on a population than the inclusion of the words 'under God' in the US Pledge of Allegiance. What were the chances I'd have found evidence of that date rather than from any of the other dates in the approximately 58,440 days of history of the house?

Perhaps I should apply the 'guiding hand' thinking. I should say 'There is no such thing as a coincidence', 'Everything happens for a reason', 'These things are meant to be'. I could say it was no coincidence that the newspaper was behind my wallpaper. Should I claim that some great Atheist force in the universe put it there to inspire me in my work? Should I say I was meant to find it?

After all, these things are meant to be. There is, of course, one other possibility. I could say that unlikely things, even 58,440 to 1 things, do sometimes happen and they are no more than chance. We could reasonably conclude that the difference between those who claim chance events are guided and those who don't is simply the difference between an irrational and rational interpretation. We could quite simply say there are such things as coincidences and they do happen. Religion, however, relies on improbable beliefs and gives permission for beliefs that make no sense but fit with their doctrine. That belief is often reinforced with emotions and a desire to believe in something or someone very special.

Chapter Twenty-Eight

FREEDOM FROM BELIEF

One of the ways in which religion is sustained is by the self-mesmerisation of prayer. A common example is the type of prayer said because a set of keys have been mislaid. A prayer is said to God or perhaps a saint to assist in the finding of them. When the keys are found, they will often be in a forgotten place, having slipped behind or off something, or had something placed on top of them. How they were lost will usually become apparent and make sense. However, the next time they are lost, there will be a memory of the prayers for them to be found. While there is no evidence that divine intervention was directly involved in finding them before, there may still be a feeling that prayer is necessary. In the anxiety of the search, there may be the fear that they will not be found if prayers are not said.

Prayer becomes a response to the anxiety of mislaid keys. The mind creates a dependency on prayer in such situations. Prayer appears to be a necessary part of the process of finding lost things.

The feelings of frustration and powerlessness over losing keys increase the effect. We tend to say things like 'How can I have been so stupid?' and berate ourselves for being careless. This contrasts with the idea that there must be a power in the universe that creates order. We want there to be a power like that as it seems like the best hope for finding the keys.

We can apply this process to many other uncertainties in life. We may have prayed to pass exams or for the success of a football team. In each case, prayer is the reflection of a desire for a powerful force that will order the world to be the way we want it.

People may, of course, pray for very noble things. I can remember as a child being part of a very large interdenominational crowd of people gathered on a school football field to pray for peace. This was in the early 1970s in Belfast. It was at a time of very intense violence. I was about ten or eleven years old and told myself that all those people praying would have an effect. How could they not? The violence carried on for many more years. There is no evidence even the most sincere and honest of prayers affect external events.

There have been attempts to try and show that prayer works in medical situations. None of these have shown any correlation between prayer and recovery. The largest and most quoted of these studies was the 'Study of the Therapeutic Effects of Intercessory Prayer (STEP)', which was led by Harvard Professor Herbert Benson and funded by the Templeton Foundation. The Templeton Foundation seeks to establish links between scientific research and spirituality. The research was carried out using a sound scientific approach with a double-blind technique and a control group.

> In the study, the researchers monitored 1,802 patients at six hospitals who received coronary bypass surgery, in which doctors reroute circulation around a clogged vein or artery.
>
> The patients were broken into three groups. Two were prayed for; the third was not. Half the patients who received the prayers were told that they were being prayed for; half were told that they might or might not receive prayers. (New York Times, 31 March 2006)

The results were not what the researchers had hoped for. They looked at major complications and the mortality rate within thirty days of the bypass. The group with the least major complications and deaths turned out to be those who were not prayed for. Fifty-one per cent of them had these serious outcomes. Those who were prayed for, but did not know it, faired very slightly worse. Fifty-two per cent of them suffered major complications or died. The group with the worst outcome were those who knew they were being prayed for. Fifty-nine per cent of them suffered these serious outcomes. Of course, those who had hoped for a different outcome derided the research. They tried to argue that prayer just wasn't amenable to that type of research, and prayer worked because they knew it worked.

This was one of a group of ten studies on the effectiveness of prayer. None of them found that prayer was effective. The same New York Times article states:

> A 1997 study at the University of New Mexico, involving 40 alcoholics in rehabilitation, found that the men and women who knew they were being prayed for actually fared worse.

These results are not enough to prove that prayer is actually harmful; however, there is certainly no evidence that it is beneficial for anything other than an act of self-direction. Alcoholics do sometimes pray not to drink today. However, a prayer like that is about building up resolution, and what power it has is to encourage the alcoholic in their own decisions. There is no evidence that any power outside of the alcoholic's own consciousness has an effect on their drinking habit. The prayer gives an incentive for sobriety. They are in effect self-fulfilling prayers. It is the desire to stay sober that is most important. The transference of that desire to a higher power does not make that higher power real.

As the tragic case of the death of an eleven-year-old girl Kara Neumann from Wisconsin shows, reliance on prayer and undue respect for such an attitude can kill. She died in 2008 from the complications arising from undiagnosed diabetes. Her parents adhered to a Pentecostal faith that did not allow medical intervention. The girl's aunt tried desperately to persuade her parents to get her help. She called the sheriff's office three times, and an ABC report records her as saying:

> My sister-in-law is, her daughter's severely, severely sick and she believes her daughter is in a coma, . . . And, she's very religious, so she's refusing to take [Kara] to the hospital, so I was hoping maybe somebody could go over there. (David Schoetz, 27 March 2008, ABC News, http://www.webcitation.org/5evCY2VzJ)

One has to wonder why her aunt had to call the authorities three times. If she'd said the child was being battered by the parents, would they have acted sooner? They didn't intervene because they didn't believe there was abuse. But where is the difference between causing a child to die violently and wilfully refusing to allow a child to have life-saving medical treatment? They did eventually seek to intervene, but the child was dead by the time they arrived.

The parents were convicted of reckless homicide. In an appeal case in 2013:

> The Neumanns' legal team argued that Wisconsin abuse laws granted criminal immunity to parents who put their faith in prayer to heal their child's ill health.
>
> But government lawyers argued that such protection ends when parents realise a child is at serious risk of death. (http://www.bbc.co.uk/news/world-us-canada-23167489)

If prayer worked as these parents apparently believed it does, God would have intervened to save their child. It is a tragic case of putting belief before human welfare. Kara was not old enough to make a free choice over her religion, but she was old enough to be the victim of her parent's belief.

One of the most harmful aspects of religion is how it infects human thought. It teaches humans to depend on the most dangerous of all vanities, that what we believe is the arbiter of truth. The implication of the lawyers arguing that the law protecting faith did not extend to a life-threatening situation is that religious faith should, as a matter of conscience, be allowed to cause harm up to that point.

Prayer is often an emotional response. There is no evidence it is a response that is heard by any supernatural being; however, there is evidence it may sometimes be a risk too far.

Chapter Twenty-Nine

MMR

As we have seen, reliance on faith can have devastating effects. The effect of the idea that belief is more important than facts ripples out from religion and causes harm elsewhere.

While the belief in horoscopes, magic crystals, and ley lines are usually pretty harmless, people deciding to put belief before evidence can have serious consequences.

In 1998, London-based surgeon and medical researcher Andrew Wakefield, along with twelve other authors, published a research paper claiming to have identified a new syndrome to which they gave the term autistic enterocolitis. They said that this raised the possibility of a link between the measles, mumps, and rubella (MMR) vaccine given to babies and the development of autism and bowel disease. The paper was published in the renowned medical journal The Lancet and was immediately controversial.

It is important to point out that the paper did not establish a causal link between MMR and autism. In spite of this, Wakefield called for the suspension of the use of the triple MMR vaccine until more research could be done. He made this call without any scientific evidence and gained a great deal of publicity by doing so. He was eventually struck off the General Medical Council (GMC) register which grants British doctors the right to practise.

> The GMC said he acted in a way that was dishonest, misleading and irresponsible while carrying out research into a possible link between the measles, mumps and rubella (MMR) vaccine, bowel disease and autism. (guardian.co.uk, Monday, 24 May 2010)

As I write this in February 2013, there is outbreak of measles in Northern England.

HPA [Health Protection Agency] North East spokeswoman, Julia Waller, said: 'This measles outbreak is very serious and we are likely to see many more cases before it's over.

'The sad thing is that most, if not all of these cases could have been avoided if people had been up-to-date with MMR vaccination.

'There are still too many children and young adults who were not vaccinated.' (http://www.bbc.co.uk, 29 January 2013)

The question I wish to address here is not why Andrew Wakefield made the claims he did, but why he was believed by so many people even after, as happened fairly quickly, top doctors, scientists, and politicians repeatedly pointed out the dangers in not giving babies the MMR vaccines. They repeatedly stated that there was no evidence for Wakefield's claims. Yet there were demonstrations in support of him. There were demands for vaccines to be administered singly (which leads to a high risk that not all injections are received). The most serious outcome was the fall in the number of babies who were vaccinated.

The problem is not simply why so many people decided to believe Andrew Wakefield instead of the evidence that doctors and scientists were presenting, but why they chose belief over evidence. I'm not saying that belief in Wakefield was a direct effect of any religion. I am saying it was the direct effect of prioritising belief over facts. For freedom from religion to be complete, it must also mean freedom from that type of thinking. For many of us who have walked away from religion, the fundamental mental freedom came when we were willing to say 'Because I believe it, does not mean it is true.' When we are willing to accept that our beliefs are not the arbiter of truth, we can begin to look at the world afresh.

Chapter Thirty

QUESTIONING BELIEF

There are two distinctly different forms of belief. The first, which applies to religious 'believers', is the acceptance of a number of claims for which no evidence has been produced. Here, 'I believe it' specifically means the acceptance of something as true where there is no evidence to show that it is. This is sometimes called having faith (though the word 'faith' does also have other meanings). This would apply to belief in the existence of God, the virgin birth, the resurrection, and many other religious beliefs.

The second type of belief is best described as having a value such as 'I believe in free speech' or 'I believe in the abolition of the death penalty'. These could often be described as principles or convictions. These differ from the first meaning of belief because they relate to things that can be shown to exist. People do get executed, and they do get locked up for expressing opinions that governments disapprove of, particularly under oppressive governments. It is easy to see that these uses of the word 'belief' are very different.

When we say we reject belief as a way of understanding the world, we mean we don't see belief as a way of deciding if a claim of fact is true. These definitions might seem like a statement of the obvious, but I have frequently encountered believers who conflate these two meanings of belief in order to assert that non-believers are as trapped in belief (accepting claims without evidence) as they are.

One of the things many religious believers argue is that beliefs are central to human life and they define what is most important. But is that true? Let's consider the very important experience of love. Think of someone you love dearly. It could be a girlfriend, boyfriend, wife, husband, parent, and so on. Now think about telling them you love them and saying, 'I believe I love you.' Saying 'I believe' would not enhance what you say. Far from it, unless it was at the stage when you were falling in love with someone, it would make it seem like you were uncertain about your feelings.

When you love someone, you just do. The language of belief is not relevant. Feelings of love are not belief; they are much deeper than anything mere belief can establish. When a mother cares for her children, it is not because she has a belief it is because she loves them. Religion may attempt to hijack that response, and in the case of the Virgin Mary, they have done so very successfully, but humans do not need a belief system in order to love their children. However, it can damage familial ties. One pattern we find in from Northern Ireland to India, and across religions around the world, is of parents rejecting a child who has married out of the religion. That is a mark of how destructive religious identity can be. What greater mark of the harm of religion can there be than that it can be stronger that the affections parents hold for their children.

Nor do the beliefs they cling to even shape our approach to the world in anything like the way that religious believers like to claim they do. From what we understand about the human mind, belief competes with fears and desires and memory, which are constantly being revised to shape our understanding of who we are. These give the idea of the 'self', but as Michael Bond puts it:

> . . . there is a growing recognition that our sense of self may be a consequence of our relationship with others 'We have this deep-seated drive to interact with each other that helps us discover who we are,' (Bruce Hood at the University of Bristol, author of The Self Illusion (Constable, 2012). New Scientist, 23 February 2013)

In this book, I have argued that the harm of religion has more to do with a sense of identity, formed in a relationship to a group, than with the individual's belief system or actions. Though religion puts claims of morality at the heart of their belief system, they have been singularly unsuccessful at preventing harmful actions such as theft and murder and have actively incited many horrific crimes throughout history.

Yet religions have thrived because they have fostered that very strong sense of identity among their believers. Beliefs clearly have an important role, but as we have seen, it is identity that shapes the beliefs rather than the identity arising from the belief. One obvious effect of this has been that there is often a strong relationship between religious and political ideas.

Religions often seek to use the political system to impose their dominance on a society. One very obvious example is sexual morality. The debate over gay marriage is raging in a number of parts of the world. One very simple way to look at this debate is as a territorial struggle. Religions see marriage as their territory. They perceive gay people as invading that territory. Territory, of course, is always very close to identity. Believers are so angry about gay marriage because they see it as threatening their Christian identity.

It is often argued that religious beliefs are no different from political ones. They are indeed often interrelated, and strongly so in some places. However, there is a significant difference. Political beliefs relate to tangible questions about the world, like who should govern the country, economic policy, or what laws should be passed. While religion might influence an individual's response to these questions, the questions themselves relate to objective reality and do not, of themselves, require faith in anything outside of objective reality.

The difference is that while no one expects politics to produce perfect answers, religion claims it can. The simplest weapon of religion is to convince believers that there has to be more than this. There has to be a powerful being who is beyond this world. There has to be a perfect destination such as Heaven or Enlightenment. In essence, religions say that there has to be something perfect somewhere and that the role of life is to reach or attain that perfect being or inner state.

This ideal of perfection has had terrible consequences for humanity. All major religions treat humanity and the human condition with a deep contempt. Christianity, Islam, and Judaism all see humanity as essentially sinful and in need of God to give them morality. Buddhism and Hinduism see humanity as ignorant and in need of a path to enlightenment. This is not to say that religions are responsible for human dissatisfaction, but that they harness and exploit it.

Freedom from religion is not, in itself, a political position. I have Twitter Followers who reject religion from across the political spectrum from right wing libertarian to Marxist viewpoints.

Chapter Thirty-One

FOOLS FOR FREEDOM

> The fool hath said in his heart, There is no God. They are corrupt,
> they have done abominable works, there is none that doeth good. (Ps. 14:1)

So the Bible condemns us for our honesty. It treats non-belief as corrupt and abominable. It demands compliance to its beliefs and doctrines and that we bow down to the image of a deity it presents. There is nothing profoundly spiritual in this. It is simply a demand to comply with a belief and an expression of hatred again those who don't. I often encounter an attitude that the rejection of religion is simply a phase people go through.

I have been repeatedly told by Christians that C.S. Lewis makes a good case against Atheism. He is held up as an example of an Atheist who saw the light and returned to Christianity, especially in his biographical work Surprised by Joy. It is in many ways a very good biography, well written and very readable. Yet this is how he described his Atheism in this work:

> I maintained that God did not exist. I was also very angry at him for
> not existing. I was equally angry at him for creating the world.

He also explains how he spent his Atheistic period enthralled by the idea of 'Northernness', his term for his interest in Norse Gods such as Odin and Thor. Yet if he was angry with God, how can he have been said to have had no belief? That is angry belief not Atheism. His account also suggests he replaced the myth of Christianity with a Norse myth. It does not suggest he ever questioned the logic of a deity's existence or fully examined the inconsistencies in the Christian myth.

Lewis returned to belief because he is moved by a remark about a 'dying God'. So his journey was one of emotional rejection of God, and he returns because of a sentimental remark. It was not a journey of reason. He, in fact, makes a contorted argument against thought being based on reason, claiming that if thought was 'subjective', it could not produce the aesthetic ideas or realise beauty. This is an assertion for which he produces no evidence and no more than a claim to support his view that humanity needs a soul. He treats the mind as a philosophical concept, rather than an evolutionary outcome. He seeks to make the mind a construction of philosophy, rather than philosophy a construction of the mind. He sees truth as either established by subjective thought or as decreed by the divine but ignores the point that the reality of the world can be established by the objective testing of facts. Yet in doing so, we accept not a fixed view of the world, but the humility of often not knowing and the honesty of not claiming there is an ultimate truth.

Christians seem to like to hold up Lewis as an example of Atheism because the self-contradictions in his position are highly obvious and his belief that there was no God proved to be highly fragile. Unfortunately, for them, many of us have a much more coherent and better thought through position than C.S. Lewis ever had.

We also have to ask ourselves why Surprised by Joy, a book that treats pederasty so lightly, is regarded as virtuous by Christians. At the school Lewis attended, younger boys were used to serve the sexual needs of older ones, and, he states he did not indulge in such activities, he treats it as no more that a minor fault. It is a puzzle why this work has for so long been a revered text of Christian apologetics.

The point of this book is not to infringe the right of the successors of Lewis to attend evensong on a pleasant summer evening with the sunlight streaming through the stained glass windows. The problem arises when those who do so declare that that should give them a right to object to gay people who want to attend an equally beautiful ceremony to get married.

The history of religion is that it has, in varying degrees, claimed ownership over people. In political terms, there has been a shift from tyranny to democracy, a journey which is far from complete but that has been the trend. The Abrahamic religions arise from an idea of tyranny. The obsessions with Hell in the New Testament and Qur'an do nothing but suggest that despite very occasional expressions of magnanimity the entry qualifications to Heaven leave no doubt that the majority will be excluded.

While writing this final chapter, I'm tweeted at by my friend the Rev. Paul Prentice, the Vicar of St Andrews Orpington. We have had a long sparring match on many things, but today we are in accord. He expresses sympathy for many of the points I make about the harm caused by religion, and I point out that I regard evensong as mostly harmless. This is a book about the harm of religion and takes that harm very seriously. It is not a book about anger against those who practise it without seeking to impose their doctrines on the rest of the world. Religion is the source of terrible harm, but Paul is a decent man with decent attitudes. When addressing religious beliefs, while I vigorously defend my position, I never make an unprovoked attack on an individual for what they believe.

Where I have addressed religion, my biggest concern has always been with the harm it causes and the right to be free from it. Some people have a moment of revelation, or perhaps I should say counter-revelation, but it is, for most, a gradual process of questioning. It may simply be a matter of one day, saying to ourselves, or others, that we no longer need this belief.

In Buddhism, there is a saying, 'Before enlightenment, chop wood and carry water. After enlightenment, chop wood and carry water.' And so it is with religion: with the exceptions of those who are harassed by unpleasant cults or religious laws, the world after religion is pretty much the same as it was before we left it. Yet walking away from religion can lead to a new approach to thought. Whereas once a beautiful sunset was evidence of a celestial being, now it is a wonder of the universe that is a so much larger concept than any God humanity can dream up.

It is claimed that belief in God is humbling and the rejection is arrogance, that we non-believers make ourselves gods. Yet where is the humility in beliefs that see humanity as the most important concern of the imagined creator of the vast universe, and where is the arrogance in saying evidence, and not what we assert to be our belief, should be the arbiter of truth?

Is God willing to prevent evil, but not able?
Then he is not omnipotent.
Is he able, but not willing?
Then he is malevolent.
Is he both able and willing?
Then whence cometh evil?
Is he neither able nor willing?
Then why call him God?
(Epicurus)

Bibliography

(Where no publisher is offered it is an out of copyright book available on Kindle)

ISAAC ASIMOV

Adding a Dimension: Seventeen Essays on the History of Science Doubleday (1964))

AYAAN HIRSI ALI

Infidel, an autobiography published in Dutch in September 2006 by publisher Augustus, Amsterdam and Antwerp, 447 pages., and in English in February 2007. Edited by Richard Miniter.
Nomad: From Islam to America: A Personal Journey Through the Clash of Civilizations, Free Press, 2010.

KAREN ARMSTRONG

Muhammad: A Biography of the Prophet, 1991.
A History of God, 1993.
Islam: A Short History, 2000.
The Battle for God: Fundamentalism in Judaism, Christianity and Islam, 2000.
Muhammad: A Prophet for Our Time, 2006.
The Case for God, 2009.

ANNE BARING AND JULES CASHFORD

The Myth of the Goddess: Evolution of an Image, Penguin Books, 1991.

SUSAN BLACKMORE

Parapsychology and Out-of-the-Body Experiences, Transpersonal Books, Hove, 1978.

Beyond the Body: An Investigation of Out-of-the-Body Experiences (1st edn.), Heinemann, London, 1982. ISBN 9780434074709;.
The Adventures of a Parapsychologist (1st edn.), Prometheus, Buffalo, NY, 1986. ISBN 9780879753603

DAN BROWN

The Da Vinci Code, 2003.

W.F. BYNUM AND ROY PORTER

Oxford Dictionary of Scientific Quotations, Oxford University Press, 2005.

CHARLES DARWIN

1844: Geological Observations on the Volcanic Islands Visited During the Voyage of H.M.S. Beagle.
1859: On the Origin of Species by Means of Natural Selection, or the Preservation of Favoured Races in the Struggle for Life.
1868: The Variation of Animals and Plants under Domestication.
1871: The Descent of Man, and Selection in Relation to Sex.
1872: The Expression of the Emotions in Man and Animals.
1880: The Power of Movement in Plants.
1881: The Formation of Vegetable Mould through the Action of Worms, with Observations on Their Habits.
1887: The Autobiography of Charles Darwin (edited by his son Francis Darwin).

RICHARD DAWKINS

(1976). The Selfish Gene, Oxford University Press, Oxford. (1982).
The Extended Phenotype: The Long Reach of the Gene, Oxford University Press, Oxford (1986).
The Blind Watchmaker, W. W. Norton, New York
(1995). River Out of Eden: A Darwinian View of Life, Basic Books, New York. (1996).
Climbing Mount Improbable, W. W. Norton, New York.
(1998). Unweaving the Rainbow: Science, Delusion and the Appetite for Wonder, Houghton Mifflin, Boston.
(2003). A Devil's Chaplain: Reflections on Hope, Lies, Science, and Love, Houghton Mifflin, Boston. (2004).
The Ancestor's Tale: A Pilgrimage to the Dawn of Evolution, Houghton Mifflin, Boston.
(2006). The God Delusion, Houghton Mifflin, Boston. ISBN 0-618-68000-4.

(2009). The Greatest Show on Earth: The Evidence for Evolution, Free Press, New York; Transworld, London. ISBN 0-593-06173-X.

(2011). The Magic of Reality: How We Know What's Really True, Free Press, New York; Bantam Press, London.

DANIEL C. DENNET

Darwin's Dangerous Idea, Evolution and the Meanings of Life, Penguin Press, 1995.

ROBIN LANE FOX

Pagans and Christians: In the Mediterranean World from the Second Century AD to the Conversion of Constantine, Viking, London, 1986.; new edition by Penguin Books, 2006. ISBN

The Unauthorized Version: Truth and Fiction in the Bible, Viking, London, 1991; new edition by Penguin Books, 2006.

JOHN FOXE

Foxe's Book of Martyrs, Ambassador Books, 2002 (first English edition 1563).

SAUL FRIEDLANDER

Memory, History, and the Extermination of the Jews of Europe, Indiana University Press, Bloomington, 1993.

Nazi Germany and the Jews: The Years of Persecution, 1933-1939, Vol. 1, HarperCollins, New York, 1997.

The Years of Extermination: Nazi Germany and the Jews, 1939-1945, HarperCollins, New York, 2007Vol.2 of the previous reference.

RICHARD ELLIOTT FRIEDMAN

Who Wrote the Bible? Jonathan Cape, 1988.

I.S. GLASS

Revolutionaries of the Cosmos: The Astro-Physicists, Oxford University Press, 2006.

CHRISTOPHER HITCHENS

1995: The Missionary Position: Mother Teresa in Theory and Practice, Verso.

2004: Love, Poverty, and War: Journeys and Essays, Thunder's Mouth, Nation Books.

2007: The Portable Atheist: Essential Readings for the Non-Believer, Perseus Publishing.

2007: God Is Not Great: How Religion Poisons Everything, Twelve/Hachette Book Group, New York/Warner Books. ISBN 0-446-57980-7/published in the UK.

2010: Hitch-22: A Memoir, Twelve. ISBN 978-0-446-54033-9. OCLC 464590644.

2011: Arguably: Essays, Twelve. UK edition as Arguably: Selected Prose, Atlantic.

WILLIAM JAMES

The Varieties of Religious Experience: A Study in Human Nature, Longmans, 1952 (original lectures 1901-2).

LAWRENCE M. KRAUSS

A Universe from Nothing: Why There Is Something Rather Than Nothing, Free Press, 2012.

KRISHNAMURTI

The Penguin Krishnamurti Reader, Penguin, 1970.

JOHN C. LENNOX

God's Undertaker: Has Science Buried God? Lion Hudson, Oxford, updated edition (1 September 2009),

The Bible & Ethics, David Gooding and John C. Lennox, Myrtlefield Trust, Ontario, 2011.

Seven Days That Divide the World: The Beginning According to Genesis and Science, John C. Lennox, Zondervan, Grand Rapids, MI (9 August 2011),

God and Stephen Hawking: Whose Design Is It Anyway? John C. Lennox, Lion Hudson, Oxford, 1st edn. (1 September 2011), 96p. ISBN 0-7459-5549-5.

Gunning for God: A Critique of the New Atheism, John C. Lennox, Lion Hudson, Oxford, 1st edn. (1 October 2011),

C.S. LEWIS

The Problem of Pain, 1940.

The Case for Christianity, 1942.

Christian Behaviour, 1943.

Miracles: A Preliminary Study, 1947 (revised 1960).

Surprised by Joy: The Shape of My Early Life, 1955 (autobiography).

DIARMAID MacCULLOCH

A History of Christianity: The First Three Thousand Years, Penguin, 2010 (first published by Allen Lane, 2009).

A.H. MASLOW

Religions, Values, and Peak-Experiences, Viking Compass, 1994 (first published by Kappa Delta, 1964).

JOSH McDOWELL

The New Evidence That Demands a Verdict, Thomas Nelson, 1999.

C. DENNIS McKINSEY

The Encyclopaedia of Bible Errancy, Prometheus Books, 1995.

RAYMOND MOODY

Life After Life: The Investigation of a Phenomenon—Survival of Bodily Death, HarperSanFrancisco, San Francisco, 2001.
Reflections on Life After Life, Stackpole Books, Harrisburg, PA, 1977.
Raymond Moody and Paul Perry, The Light Beyond, Bantam Books, New York, 1988.
Raymond Moody and Paul Perry, Glimpses of Eternity: Sharing a Loved One's Passage from This Life to the Next, Guideposts, New York, 2010.
Raymond Moody and Paul Perry, Reunions: Visionary Encounters with Departed Loved Ones, Villard Books, New York, 1993.

JAMES ORR

The Christian View of God and the World, 1893.
God's Image in Man and Its Defacement in the Light of Modern Denials (1905).

ELAINE PAGELS AND KAREN L.KING

Reading Judas The controverval Message of the Ancient Gospel of Judas Penguin Books 2007.

GAVIN PRETOR-PINNEY

The Wavewatcher's Companion, Bloomsbury, 2010.

SALMAN RUSHDIE

The Satanic Verses, Viking, 1988.

J. ANDERSON THOMSON, JR., WITH CLARE AUKOFER

Why We Believe in God(s): A Concise Guide to the Science of Faith, Pitchstone Publishing, 2011.

EVELYN UNDERHILL

Mysticism: A Study in the Nature and Development of Spiritual Consciousness, Dover Publications, 2002 (first published 1930).
Practical Mysticism, Dover Publications, 2000 (first published 1915).

JAMES D. WATSON

The Double Helix: A Personal Account of the Discovery of the Structure of DNA, Folio Society (first published by Orion Publishing 1968).

'SACRED' TEXTS

THE HOLY BIBLE

King James Version
Scofield references (originally 1909), text translated 1611, date of original text, highly disputed.
English Standard Version translated 1971.

Tanakh (Tanach)

Jewish Bible (1917 Jewish Publication Society Translation) by Jewish Publication Society and Max Margolis (26 May 2011).

THE HOLY QUR'AN

Translated by Abdullah Yusuf Ali, Wordsworth, 2000.

OTHER SCRIPTURES

The Dead Sea Scrolls The Folio Society 2000.
The Lost Books of the Bible, Testament Books, 1979.
The Nag Hammadi Scriptures, edited by Marvin Meyer, HarperOne, 2007.

Index